Bev Spicer i
Amazon, whi
reviews. She
the name of Bev Spicer) and mystery/suspense (under the name of B. A. Spicer). 'Bunny on a Bike' has been in the Amazon Best Sellers lists for *Humour* and *Memoir*. She graduated from Queens' College Cambridge with a PGCE and taught English in many countries before returning to Cambridge and taking up a teaching post at Anglia Ruskin University. She now writes full-time and lives in France with her husband and two youngest children.

MW01288790

Other titles by Bev Spicer

'One Summer in France' (two girls in a tent)
'Bunny on a Bike' (Playboy croupiers in 80s London)

Titles by B. A. Spicer

'My Grandfather's Eyes' (dark, psychological drama)
'A Good Day for Jumping' (mystery and suspense on the island of Crete)
'The Undertaker's Son' (mystery and suspense in France)
'Angels' (a metaphysical short story)
'Strings, and other disturbing stories' (available September 2014)

Stranded in the Seychelles

by
Bev Spicer

Cover Design

by
Sue Michniewicz

Contents

Milton Keynes or the Seychelles?

Older but not wiser, we perused the Times Educational Supplement for jobs, on a dull afternoon in August at my house in Milton Keynes. Carol was back, and suddenly, living in Milton Keynes didn't seem to matter as much. My bosom buddy had spent the previous year working in a school in the Himalayas, and had finally flown back to somewhere nearer sea level.

Outside, nothing was happening. Inside, the walls remained perfectly aligned and painted magnolia. Carol sighed and looked out of the large, double-glazed window onto a square patch of lawn penned in by a chest-high, cheap, wooden fence. "How can you live in a place called Pennyland?"

As I didn't know the answer to this question, I hedged. "It's only a name."

"It's a stupid name."

I had to admit that Carol was right. It couldn't have helped that she had been used to living in a mountaintop retreat in Tibet, above the clouds and as remote as you can get from affordable housing, inadequate porches and gas central heating.

"How do you stand it?"

"It's not that bad," I said, half-heartedly.

A man cycled past. "Christ! It's worse than science fiction!"

Baffled as I was by this particular insight, I laughed, and Carol gave me a look that I recognised instantly. It was a look that said it was time to set out again into the world, united against the banal, the drab and the superficial, determined to have some fun and wreak some havoc. I went back to the newspaper and kicked off with something contentious:

"There's one here for a maths teacher in Beijing. I could be the stay-at-home housewife."

"No thanks," replied Carol.

"Too much of a culture shock? Don't want the Saturday morning military training?"

"Nah. Can't stand Chinese food. All those wriggly bits. And oyster sauce – can't eat oysters since Alice!"

"In Wonderland?"

"Yeah."

"The Walrus and the Carpenter?"

"The very same. Poor little oysters…"

I realised that, cartoon horror apart, and allowing for Carol's sketchy knowledge of proper Chinese cuisine, this would be a deal-breaker. Food was top priority, followed closely by sunshine, a great beach and a good library. Good looking, intelligent men of independent means were also a consideration.

"No blokes there, either. Too short. Too Chinese."

I could not argue, although I would not have put my feelings in quite the same way. Carol spoke her mind, whilst I generally harboured my sharp-edged opinions. I didn't mention the fact that, this time, she was indulging in a stereotypical assessment of a nation containing over one hundred million people, not all of whom would be too short or, indeed, too Chinese.

"What about this one?" I suggested. "*English teachers required by the Seychelles government.* Sounds interesting."

"Aren't they in the Indian Ocean?" Carol sat back in her chair and poked a finger into her ear. She was as beautiful as ever. How I had missed her!

"I believe that is correct, you lovely tart," I replied, pretty sure that Carol knew a lot more about the Seychelles than she was letting on.

"Capital?" she asked.

"Mahé."

"Climate?"

"Tropical."

"Food?"

"Fish. Creole style."

"Chips?"

"I think it's more likely to be rice," I said, although I wasn't entirely sure.

"Fish and rice with curry sauce!"

"We can make our own chips," I said, reasonably. "Just need a chip pan and some Trex."

"Granted." Carol chewed the pencil we were using to circle ads. It had also served as a coffee spoon and more recently, to kill an ant.

"Shall I read the rest of it?"

"Don't see why not," she said.

"*The National Youth Service of the Seychelles seeks-* "

"The National *what*!"

"Youth Service. Must be something like the Department of Education."

"Doesn't *sound* like the Department of Education. Go on. Let's hear it."

"*The National Youth Service of the Seychelles seeks qualified teachers of ESL to instruct secondary school students on the island of Ste. Anne.*"

"Never heard of it. There's Mahé and Praslin and some kind of bird island. Let me see." Carol grabbed the paper. "*Twelve-month contracts. Flights and accommodation provided. Interviews to be held in London on 14th/15th August.*" She closed the newspaper, discarding it on the sofa, and got up. "Want a cuppa?"

I followed my friend into the kitchen, thinking that the interviews would be at the end of the week, in three days' time.

"Where d'you keep the biscuits, you bugger? Hope you're not still buying those Poptarts!" Carol was opening cupboards, rummaging.

"There are some Jammy Dodgers in the cutlery drawer," I told her. The mention of Poptarts had brought back a momentary nostalgia.

She eyed me and I eyed her back.

"Are we going?" I asked.

"Book it, Danno," she said.

We were not the kind of girls to pass up an opportunity like this. We had been through university together and worked for Playboy in London, as blackjack dealers. After that, Carol had left England to sell encyclopaedias in

Germany and had thrown it in after meeting a businessman at a party who offered her a job teaching English to Buddhist monks in the Himalayas. I had gone on to work as a secretary in London at various establishments which were practised in the art of exploiting as little as possible of a person's potential and where, at my lowest ebb, I had slavishly typed out legal contracts for solicitors who patronised both their staff and their clients. Later, I had worked for a very nice family with a business just off Oxford Street, in a small office, up some rickety stairs, where I had learned all there was to know about high-tensile low-density bin bags (didn't take long), including how to fold them and label them, before sending them off with a quote for anything from a couple of hundred to tens of thousands. And, after just over a year of knowing that I didn't want to be in plastic for the rest of my days, I had applied for and, to my utter amazement, been accepted by Queens' College to do a postgraduate teaching certificate at Cambridge University. I subsequently took up my first post in Milton Keynes, where I discovered that I was no good at controlling a class of secondary school kids who didn't care about Keats, and I gradually came to realise that the next proper adventure was long overdue. All I had needed was the return of my best friend and sparring partner.

Carol had descended from the mountains under slightly mysterious circumstances, which she refused to divulge, but which had probably involved some kind of extra-curricular activity with one of her students. She had telephoned me to say that she wanted to come and stay for a while. So, with my probationary year as a very eager, but more or less ineffectual English teacher at Stantonbury Campus mercifully completed, and with no one begging me to stay, there was nothing to stop us, apart from fear of the unknown and crushing financial limitations. We were in the market for some excitement and risk. A teaching job in the Indian Ocean, with all expenses paid, seemed an opportunity too good to miss.

We looked up trains to London and, in the meantime, found out that the Seychelles was a group of volcanic and coral islands stuck in the middle of nowhere, with a language that was based on French, due to the fact that they had been colonised by... France. Following this, the islands had been subjected to British rule, before gaining independence in 1976. I wondered vaguely whether we would be welcomed by the locals, until Carol pointed out that anything 'we' had done to them was bound to be better than the treatment they would have received at the hands of our closest allies, the French, who, according to Carol, had used the inhabitants as slaves to work on their plantations and probably taught them to roll their Rs.

I dialled the number in the advertisement and asked to be put through to Roseline Bananne.

An Indian Ocean Interview

I can't remember the name of the hotel in London where the interviews took place, but I do recall being singularly unimpressed by it. The receptionist was pleasant enough, and politely directed us to an office several floors up before going back to rolling her eyes while she chatted on the phone to her friend.

"Maybe we could get hotel jobs," suggested Carol, as the elevator numbers lit up.

"Looks boring," I replied.

"Be all right for a while."

"Trust me on this one. I've got experience of being stuck behind a counter, gazing out at the world, waiting for five o'clock."

"When was this? Do tell."

I ignored the sarcasm and answered the question. "Sixth form. Sketchley's. Saturday job. Ugh!"

"Sounds uninspiring. Whoever would have thought it!" Carol made faces in the mirror and checked her teeth for bits.

"Pinning tickets on men's trousers was the worst."

"Any highlights at all?"

"Sewing on buttons," I mused, consumed by an unexpected nostalgia for the smell of dry cleaning fluids and the blast of steam presses.

"Doesn't sound very tempting… Did they appreciate your sewing skills?"

"Anything beat being on the shop floor – I felt so trapped behind the huge window looking out onto the High Street crammed with free people."

"Like a moth?"

"Eh?"

The slow-moving lift juddered to a halt as I did my best to make sense of the mixed metaphors, and Carol zoomed off, doing one of her silly, regal walks.

We waited in a small, violently lit room with a couple of other much younger applicants, who were evidently overcome by our apparent sangfroid, and were obviously too afraid to strike up a conversation, in case they discovered they had less to offer than we did. Doing nothing to disabuse them of their erroneous assumptions, we lowered ourselves gracefully into the low-slung, low-cost, vinyl seating, which emitted a short but ambiguous puff of air.

Before long, we were called into an even smaller room with no windows, where a man from the Seychelles National Youth Service welcomed us with a grin that seemed both inappropriate and unnerving. He was around forty, with curly, greying hair and sun-ruined skin that had once been European. He was motionless in a way that inspired curiosity – I wanted to prod him. Perhaps this was part of the interview selection process. Perhaps those candidates who showed initiative would be recruited.

Our host remained static and inscrutable. We would later learn that the Seychelles was a place where an overwhelming majority of people shifted position as little as possible, and had no concept of anything being urgent, or even necessary. When the silence had gone on for long enough to make us giggle, our interviewer came out of standby mode and subtly re-activated.

"Bev and Carol, isn't it?" he murmured, still grinning, not standing or holding out a hand.

We confirmed who we were and waited for him to tell us his name and/or ask us to sit down.

"I'm John," he said, eventually, as though this was all we needed to hear to know everything about him.

Carol nudged me and we each pulled out a chair.

"You are both teachers?"

"Yes."

"Ah, yes. Do you have your certificates?"

We did. Mine was a full teaching qualification and Carol's was a twelve-week TEFL diploma. John pushed the papers inside a folder without so much as a glance. He began speaking, as though from a script.

"The children speak English as a second language, as you probably already know. The school day and syllabus is modelled on the British system. They study a range of subjects, including English and Maths, and learn to be responsible members of society. There are two campuses, both of them based on the island of Ste. Anne."

I was touched by the way he'd referred to the students as children. He obviously had not taught a group of teenagers in a confined space.

"How do we get to the school?" Carol asked.

John considered how to answer, obviously wrong-footed by Carol's practical concerns.

"Do we live on the island?" I prompted.

John looked away from Carol and smiled at me. "You will cross from Mahé to Ste. Anne by boat."

This was pretty obvious, and I felt that we had slipped up slightly, so I ploughed in with something more pertinent.

"Do you have a syllabus for us to look at?"

John showed what I presumed to be professional empathy by raising one eyebrow, a skill I had never mastered. I wondered whether he could wiggle his ears as well.

"When would the contract begin?" asked Carol with a small sigh.

"You would start teaching in September and we would fly you out a week early, so that you could settle into your accommodation and meet the other teachers."

He gazed at us for a while and we gazed back. I pictured a luxury villa on the beach, fresh coconut for breakfast, bananas coming at me from all directions. I would live in bikinis and sarongs, cutting a fresh bloom from my tropical garden to pop behind my ear each morning. Carol would make tea and insist on a toaster. Would there be toasters in the Seychelles? I pondered this sudden concern for a moment. Meanwhile, John had either fallen asleep with his eyes open, or was reading my mind.

I waited patiently, wondering if we had made any impression whatsoever. It was difficult to know whether we were the kind of people he was looking for. In the end, it always came down to whether someone liked you or not. That's just how it is, was, and always will be. If you weren't the right kind of person, your qualifications and experience were of little or no importance. I considered telling him that we had worked for Playboy, but Carol, who was an accomplished mind reader, kicked me under the table. I scowled and she shook her head.

John came to with a smile, but didn't seem to have any more questions for us, and once again, we waited for what would happen next. It was the strangest interview I had ever had and I was pretty sure that Carol was thinking the same thing.

After what seemed to be a moment of transcendental enlightenment, which involved a rigorous re-animation of his left eyebrow, John said that the jobs were ours if we wanted them, and handed us a wad of papers, which contained what he called *essential information*. If we agreed to the terms of the contract, we could go ahead and book our flight using the coupons provided.

It wasn't really a tough decision. If we stayed in England, I would go mad, attempt to throttle Jimmy Lockley and Mary Walters (two of my most psychopathic students) and probably end up behind bars. Carol would marry Dave for want of something better to do, which would be a tragedy for both of them, and disastrous for me. We hadn't finished being young. Carol was twenty-nine and I was thirty. We wanted to see some more of the world, preferably for free, and definitely travel as far away as possible from Milton Keynes.

With a final glance at each other, the deal was done.

"Where do we sign?" asked Carol.

"On the dotted line," said John. There was that smile again, and in his eyes we saw genuine pleasure.

Hey presto! Seychelles here we come!

Bemused and delighted, we walked past the other candidates, boarded the grotty lift and danced our way down to the ground floor, past the still yapping receptionist and out into the London smog. What an adventure we were about to have!

"Time for a celebratory cream cake extravaganza!" cried Carol.

It was a tradition. It would be messy. It was just what we needed.

Leaving on a Jet Plane

I awoke to yet another grey day in August. Another failed summer. All the more reason to bail out and disappear from the land of drizzle. We had travelled north, to Carol's parents' house near Sheffield, and, at present, I was trying to drive my orange camper van into her dad's meticulously organised garage, where it would be stored safely away until we came back.

"That's it. Just watch out for the bike. Keep going. Easy does it. Stop!"

The van was too high. Carol's dad hadn't been expecting the crunch to come from above.

"Bugger!" he said, standing there in his fawn cardigan.

"Dad!" said Carol.

"What's happened?" said Mrs. Baker, hurrying out of the house wiping her hands on a floral tea towel and looking concerned, in startling red lipstick.

"Hello, Mrs. Baker," I said, leaning out of the driver's window. "Nice lippy!"

"Nothing to worry about, dear," said Mr. Baker, scowling.

"Thank you, Beverley," replied Mrs. Baker, pouting a little. "Cherry Passion. The Pound Shop."

"Very fetching!"

"*I* thought so. What was that bang I heard? It sounded very loud."

"Nothing serious, dear," said Mr. Baker, again.

"You've hit the garage roof!" observed Carol's mum.

"Not to worry," her husband said, looking worried.

"We could let the tyres down," suggested Carol.

After a moment's stunned silence, we all agreed that this was an inspired idea, and half an hour later, the roof of the van cleared the entrance to the garage and rolled back until it smashed into the skylight.

"Bugger and blast!" said Mr. Baker.

Our suitcases were in the boot of the Bakers' gleaming family saloon, and Carol's mum handed us an unfeasibly large Tupperware containing sardine sandwiches, a flask of tea and a small tin of butterfly cakes. She hugged us both and told us to take care, looking weepy and a little crumpled, as we climbed into the car and strapped on our seatbelts.

I felt a lightness in my stomach and a strong sense of expectation as we backed out of the driveway, listening to Carol's dad telling us about his first ever teaching job in Birmingham. The journey would seem a lot longer than it was. I opened up the cake tin and stuffed a butterfly into my mouth.

Carol turned on the radio, but all the stations were pre-set for Jazz, dead comedians or sports news.

"I've got some Mozart of your mother's in the centre console," he offered.

Mozart turned out to be Vivaldi. The Four Seasons never sounded so good.

We were flying from Heathrow. Carol navigated and Mr. Baker reluctantly followed his daughter's directions, rolling his eyes at me in the rear-view mirror. Of course, we arrived in the right place at more or less the right time and he was forced to admit that Carol had done a sterling job.

"Not bad at all!" said Mr. Baker. "Chip off the old block!"

"Thanks for the lift, Dad."

"Will you be all right from here?"

"Thanks for the lift, Mr. Baker."

And, after we had unloaded our gear, we watched him drive away.

"Your dad's very nice," I said.

"Terrible bigot, bit of a racist, mental control freak, but I digress… Where are the tickets?"

"You had them."

"No, I didn't."

"Yes, you did. They're in your bum bag."

"What bum bag?"

"The one you were wearing round your waist," I blurted.

I searched under my jumper, in random panic. Then, I noticed that the tickets were in her hand. She'd had them all the time.

"Absolute dunderhead!"

And, just like that, Carol had got me. Hook line and sinker. Extremely childish. Old habits die hard.

Having never been in a jumbo jet before, it was a revelation to me that so many people could fly in one plane, all at the same time. There was a central aisle of four seats, with three more either side. I thought about attempting a calculation and decided against it. The fuselage was huge. But what struck me most, after we had taken off, laboriously climbing into the sky in accordance with the laws of thermodynamics but against all reasonable logic, was the atmosphere of complete disarray. People jumped up, children ran wild, lights flashed on and made that sound that always reminds me of mental institutions or the panic-free 'siren' at Center Parcs when someone had dashed their brains out on the death slide and no one was supposed to know except the staff.

The hostesses came tottering with drinks, baby's bottles, pillows, bowls of cornflakes, champagne. It was impossible to settle, and sleeping would require accessories that we had not thought to bring with us.

"Want to watch a film?" suggested Carol.

"What is there?"

"Top Gun?"

"Seen it."

"Witness?"

"Seen it."

"Dirty Rotten Scoundrels."

"Who's in it?"

"Michael Caine and Steve Martin."

An easy decision.

That took care of a couple of hours and one more to enact the funniest lines and snicker together. For the remaining seven we tried to read, tried to sleep and talked about what might be waiting for us when we got off the plane. We ate the food we were given with enthusiasm and collected morsels from our more discerning neighbours, happy to subsidise the tiny portions.

"I wonder what it's like in First Class," said Carol, sticking her tongue out at a little girl two rows forward who was refusing to eat her apple. "Got any ear plugs?"

It turned out that you could get earplugs from the hostess for a pound. That passed a few minutes, as did inserting them in several different ways before finding out they didn't work. Eventually, though, Carol fell asleep on my shoulder and I closed my eyes, dreaming of white sand and coral reefs, tropical fish and exotic birds, Sting and Harrison Ford.

I suppose I slept for a good while because the next thing I knew was that the captain was announcing our imminent arrival. Just then, the little girl Carol had tormented earlier, who had obviously still not eaten her apple, launched it in our direction. A lucky shot - it bounced off Carol's headrest and rolled onto the floor. Had my dearest pal not been asleep on my shoulder it would have been a direct hit. The girl grinned and sat down. I woke Carol and she screamed,

"We're under attack! Down periscope! Dive! Dive!"

"We're landing. Put your seat belt on," I said, gently, picturing Richard Basehart's concerned expression, as Seaview plunged into a steep descent to avoid a giant squid. We shared the same television history, after all.

Juliette's Tre-byen Poolet

When we stepped off the plane, it was like stepping into a convection oven. There were no pockets of cooler air, just a homogenous suffocation of heat. What was more, the high humidity made ordinary breathing a skill. We stared around us and I wondered whether it would always be like this, or whether it might simply be the blast of the engines, the tarmac, or the beginning of a disaster movie about accelerated global warming.

"Christ on a bike!" said Carol. "It's like being inside the tropical house at the Botanical Gardens."

I could add no more. The logical simplicity and truth of her pronouncement overwhelmed me. We were in the biggest botanical gardens ever, with no hope of finding an exit. As I pondered this awful reality in the temporary oasis of the air-conditioned airport building, handing over passports and waiting for luggage to arrive on the carrousel, I began to realise that there may be other equally unattractive aspects of tropical life that we hadn't taken into account. Perhaps we would always be moist, our hair lank, our feet prone to athlete's foot. Perhaps our lungs would fill up with water and slowly drown us.

"We're in the Seychelles!" cried Carol, grabbing her suitcase, then me, and jumping up and down on the spot, causing a ripple of low-level excitement and a painful jarring sensation in my spine.

A man came warily towards us. It was our extremely sweaty and, after a moment's hesitation, very friendly driver, who spoke only Creole, which I could barely make out, as its resemblance to French eluded me initially. He laughed, shook his head, nodded and drove with a total disregard for the rules of the road (if, indeed, there were any), dropping us off at a colonial-style bed and breakfast, where a woman of mixed race and bad genes met us at the gate, uttered a well-aimed, scathing reprimand to our driver, and received an equally disrespectful-sounding reply. Having looked Carol and I up and down, she stuck her chin out, sniffing loudly, and whisked us inside, confiscating our passports and showing us to a sweltering room with two single beds in it, both draped with grimy mosquito nets. There was no air conditioning. She wanted to know when we would eat.

"Tell her to go away," muttered Carol. "I want to sleep. What time is it, anyway?"

"Lunchtime," said our host, briskly. "Now! Lunchtime." She remained standing in the doorway, her arms folded resolutely, wearing the expression of a suspicious and petulant toddler.

"Would it be all right if we rested?" I asked, tentatively. "Perhaps we could sleep for a while and have dinner later?"

"Dinner! I call you. All right." Her bulky hips moved alarmingly under her floral dress.

Carol and I lay down on our beds and more or less passed out in the heat, only to be woken later by a blazing row outside our window.

"Keep it down!" shouted Carol, half asleep.

I sat up, still groggy from the journey and the heat, and through the netted window in the electrically lit darkness, was able to make out our hostess, brandishing what seemed to be a broom of sorts at a wiry, dark-skinned man in shorts and shirt. The man cowered, not answering back, as the woman's insults rained down on him, along with numerous sharp thwacks from her weapon of choice, as she moved forward and brought the broom down around his head and shoulders.

Carol sat up, rubbing her eyes and craning her neck. "Bloody hell! What's she doing to the poor sod. Oi! Stop that!" She got up and lumbered over to bang on the window.

The woman hesitated, looking round and smiling pleasantly, as though nothing untoward were happening. The man bent quickly to pick up his hat, which had fallen to the ground during the attack, and backed away, receiving one last blow to his shoulders and another verbal volley from our landlady, before she turned once more and beckoned sweetly to us, first setting the broom against the wall of a shed into which the man had disappeared.

"Blimey! Must be her husband," said Carol, picking up a small, rough-looking towel and going into the bathroom.

"Do you think so?"

It seemed unlikely. For one thing, they were obviously of different race, he being of African descent and she of Malaysian or perhaps Chinese. For another, she was older than he was and obviously of greater social standing.

"I think it must be the gardener," I said.

"Nah! If it were, he wouldn't stand for it! Must be the husband."

I pondered the implications of this, picturing Dave pursued by Carol plus pitchfork. I didn't want to tell Carol that, in the Seychelles, marriage was uncommon; that it was a matriarchal society, where men cruised between women, propagating lazily and then sloping off to drink South African sherry and catch fish when they got hungry.

"I could eat a scabby horse!" announced my dearest friend, prophetically, now sporting a white cotton dress and flashy sandals.

"Nicely turned out for din-dins, my lovely."

"Cheers. Armpits were rank!"

"I'll just have a wash and be with you in a minute."

Needless to say, when I came back to the bedroom to slip on a rather fetching pink button-through number, teamed with sparkly platform mules, Carol was nowhere to be seen. Her sudden desertions were something I'd become used to over the years.

I went out, noticing with relief that there was a solid lock on our door, but wondering why we had been given no key. Our room was at the back of the house, so I made a couple of turns before recognising the gate we had entered when we'd first arrived. I couldn't help glimpsing the beaten man, who now appeared to be very much the paid help, as he tipped his hat and lowered his eyes with a reverence that almost made me laugh, until I understood that his obsequious bearing was an intentional politeness.

Carol was in the dining room, sitting at a table in the company of a man dressed in conspicuously washed and ironed clothes, sporting a baseball cap.

"Hi. I'm Mike." He stood and touched my hand, rather than shaking it. It was very clammy. He was not tall, had very short hair, rectangular glasses and an American accent. He looked around thirty-five, older than us and delighted, it seemed, to have female company.

"Mike's staying here too," said Carol.

"Right," I said, smiling. "I'm Bev."

"Nice to meet you, Bev, Carol. What d'you girls think of the place?"

It was difficult to know the extent of his enquiry. Did he mean the country or the establishment in which we were holed up? More to the point, had he just addressed us as 'girls'?

"Haven't been here long," I replied, while Carol ate the last piece of some not very appetising-looking grey bread from a tiny basket.

"Mike's in the Marines," Carol informed me. At least, that's what I thought she said.

"Really?"

"On leave. Got a friend in the south of the island. Going over there day after tomorrow."

Our hostess arrived and Mike spoke to her in Creole. She giggled like a schoolgirl. She brought paw paw, pink and sweet, sprinkled with ginger, followed by a pan of steaming stew, giving off a curry-like aroma. We ate together, in a sort of communal lucky dip, fishing around for bits of meat and vegetables.

"What d'you make of Juliette?" asked Mike, pulling out a chicken wing with a morsel of meat dangling from it.

"Oh," I said, thinking the name wholly inappropriate for a woman in her fifties with a pockmarked face and impressive biceps. "She seems quite violent."

Mike exploded, and Juliette, looking alarmed, nearly came over, until he smiled, wiping his mouth with a napkin and waving her away. "No, Juliette. *Sa va. Sa va. Tre-byen.*"

"She was giving her husband a hard time earlier," said Carol, pulling out the remnants of a chicken thigh from the less than sumptuous Seychellois dish. "Not much meat on this, is there?"

Mike laughed again. "That's not her husband. That's Maurice. Security guard and general dog's body. Lower caste, so she beats him. That's the way it is here."

We finished our meal, listening to Mike, hearing about the island and wondering who his friend was, whether it was a native girl, whether he had one in every port.

Juliette eventually arrived to clear away the dishes, suddenly flirtatious again in Mike's company.

"Nice chicken, Juliette. *Tre bon gou*."

She grinned, showing a surprisingly good set of teeth, and winked lecherously at Mike.

"Thought I recognised it from last night. Don't remember leaving much on it."

At this accusation, she tutted, shaking her head, but maintaining the girlish grin mercifully reserved for her male guest.

"Don't think it'll stretch a third night. Eh, Juliette? *Poolet fini*!"

Juliette shook her head in earnest now, understanding enough to know that her thrifty trick had been rumbled. "No, no! *Pa mem poolet*! Different. I kill special for you." She twisted her hands against each other to demonstrate the manner in which she had executed the new bird.

"She's a canny old fox," said Mike, when she had retreated, helping himself to a toothpick.

Carol belched delicately and I stared at what looked like an enormous cockroach moving quickly towards the kitchens.

We told Mike why we had come to the island, as we sat together on the veranda after dinner, drinking *Seybrew* – the local beer. He said that education was 'big' in the Seychelles, having been made free to all in the early 1980's.

"Most kids nowadays can read and write," he told us, "but their parents, well, they can sign their name. That's about it."

"Bugger me," said Carol, which made Mike laugh.

"What about the government? Isn't it socialist?" I asked, tentatively, not wanting to betray my ignorance too much.

"Working towards it, but capitalism will arrive sooner or later, even in paradise."

Mike told us that the government was still evolving, that René had his enemies, and that it was likely there would be more trouble. A one party state could never be a democracy, he declared. A communist dictatorship was what it was at the moment, and that meant a free market economy would take its time to surface. The problem was that, in the meantime, people with prospects were leaving.

After a few more beers, things became muddled, and I was glad when he put serious politics aside. I liked it more when he spoke with affection about the Seychellois people, describing them as unspoiled, fun-loving, but easily exploited. South Africa was the nearest 'civilised' country and most of the hotels on the islands belonged to wealthy businessmen. Beneath the surface, there was prostitution, small-scale drug dealing and money laundering. It should have been no surprise to us, but it was. Mike was a 'man of the world', a realist. His views were interesting and his manner sufficiently humble. The future of the Seychelles was a subject close to his heart.

We talked well into the night, cooler now, and under a sky never before so bright with stars, taking in as much as we could and doing our best to understand the history and the politics of the islands.

Mike said goodnight first, and assured us that we were magnanimous people, better than he, arriving to take part in the education of the students who were the future of the island, its life's blood. He was so drunk that, when he stood to go to his room, he stumbled, laughing and calling something out to Juliette about the beer, accusing her of putting something in it so that she could creep into his room and take advantage of him.

For all we knew, it could have been true.

Reptiles and Snoozing Spiders

The National Youth Service had taken on other teachers, some British, a couple of French, a handful of Swiss and a girl from the neighbouring island of Mauritius. A meeting was called at Head Office, and we were collected by taxi, deposited in a modern, rather uninspiring building and shown some slides of the island of Ste. Anne, featuring a group of presentable students going about their daily tasks. Not only did they study, but they were responsible for cooking, cleaning and even growing some of the food they ate. The uniforms they wore were brown and cream, finished with red scarves. The timetable was British, with lessons in the morning beginning at nine and continuing in the afternoon until four. I thought the girls looked like happy but exhausted Brownies. What struck me most was the setting: lush palms, dramatic skies and sunshine. We really were living in the middle of a tropical rain forest.

At the beginning of term, enormous, majestic schooners came, with bright, billowing sails, to bring the children they had collected from their island homes to resume their education. An education provided by the government. An education for all. I wondered how it felt for these children to be away from their families, marooned for twelve weeks at a time, in a place that represented opportunity, the promise of a better life. There were no mobile phones in those days;

communication would be a slow process. The faces that we saw on the slide projections were brave, almost heroic, but I couldn't help noticing something simmering behind the jolly, robust smiles.

Education was good for them, we were proudly informed. Education was the key to the future of the islands. The boys and girls were privileged and would strive to do their best. Like all propaganda, some of the enthusiasm sounded just a little hollow.

"Boarding school in the Indian Ocean. Who would have thought it?" muttered Carol. "Fancy!"

"It looks a bit basic," I replied.

"The kids will be all right, I reckon. "

"Do you think they like it?"

"Like going to school? Did you? Does anyone?" Carol always knew how to put things into context.

The slide show was over and the next subject on the agenda was teacher accommodation. For a moment, I worried that we would be sent to Ste. Anne to live alongside our students, but this fear was soon allayed.

We were offered a choice of housing, all of which was situated on the main island, Mahé. There was Beau Vallon, with its bungalows on the beach, Belvedere, away from the coast, in the north, and Anse à la Mouche on the coast in the south of the island, where the houses were more substantial, with large balconies and air-conditioning.

Penny and Richard, Yorkshire folk, immediately opted for Beau Vallon beach, hands raised and dead sure. We decided to have a look at the south of the island, despite the fact that it would mean a longer journey to work. I had a feeling that our choice of neighbours would be important.

We did, however, have the opportunity to visit Beau Vallon first, as Penny and Richard had already been given their keys and we were curious. It was idyllic. It was hard to believe that the arc of, admittedly, basic one-storey buildings were largely at the disposal of the employees of The National Youth Service. Teacher accommodation had never looked so attractive in terms of location. Now, I see that the place has become a high-end tourist resort, although some of the online reviews suggest that the facilities may not have been updated much.

"What shall we do?" I asked Carol, looking out to sea and feeling the warm sand between my toes.

"It would be good here, if it weren't for that!" replied Carol.

Penny's voice was a monotonous drawl, as she ordered Dick around, in tones of sarcastic familiarity that would inevitably lead to murder of one kind or another.

"South, then?" I suggested.

"Anse à la Mouche, it is!"

"Did you know that *mouche* means *fly*?" I told her.

"Yeah. It also means *bogey*. I looked it up."

"What does *Anse* mean?"

"*Intestinal loop, bay* or *cove*."

"Mmm. *Bogey Cove* – great address!"

Penny had snuck up on us.

"It means *Windy Bay.* We asked John." This was Penny, trying to be friendly; perhaps we should give her more of a chance. Perhaps we were abominable human beings. I considered the roundness of her face, her mass of freckles and curly red hair. She *looked* friendly enough. I searched for a moment of connection, but empathy was strangely absent between us. She smirked and I shuddered.

"Dick! You've left the microwave on the veranda! Make some tea for everyone when you've moved it!" She smiled unappealingly at Carol and I, presuming no doubt that we were as one. Women united. Feminists, doggedly assertive, bent on the oppression of men.

"He's well behaved most of the time," she added, banging yet another nail into her coffin. I visualised the idiom unsuccessfully.

"Had a dog called Richard years ago," said Carol, out of the blue, her expression as sober as I'd ever seen it.

"What kind?" asked Penny, with a laugh to match her irritating personality.

"A spaniel. Useless around the house. Had it put down."

Penny didn't get it. What she didn't get, she ignored. "D'you take sugar? Better go and make sure he's got the kettle on."

We said we didn't take sugar, quietly appalled that all the signs we were blaring out at her had been missed. It was a friendship that would never get very far, and, as Penny marched off up the beach like a disgruntled hippo, towards the open door behind which Dick was presumably cowering, I knew that even our shared affinity for this island paradise would not be enough to unite us. Anse à la Mouche, windy or not, suddenly seemed the only sensible option.

"Did you really have a dog called Richard?" I asked.

"What do you think, you dope?"

"Well, my friend had a goldfish called Elizabeth, so it seemed possible, that's all."

Carol grinned. She liked the idea of a goldfish called Elizabeth.

"Are you missing Dave?" I asked, after a moment, seeing something in her bearing, as we watched the movement of the sea and scanned the horizon.

"A bit. Not much."

"A year is a long time. Do you think he'll –"

"– wait? 'Course he will!"

"I was going to say, do you think he'll come out to see you?"

"Nah. Told him not to. Better to leave it for a while."

I remembered *Camping La Belle Sirène*, where we had spent a glorious study break as part of our degree course at University. So did Carol. Dave's visit had been a disaster. The Seychelles experience would be better without him. And, with this thought, I stifled the cruel realisation that this could very well be our final adventure.

Penny appeared at the door of the bungalow, waving and screeching.

"We'd better go and have some tea and defend Dick for a bit," I said.

"Then we'll go," answered Carol, simply.

"Good thinking, Batman." I hadn't planned to say it. It had just popped out. It was another blast from the past. Carol let me off with a deprecating sneer and a pinch. If I'd grinned any more widely, I'd have hurt myself.

We spent another hour or so, trying to get to know Dick a little. It turned out that he was more or less insufferable too, having been more or less subsumed by his all-powerful wife – they were married, we learned. After we had heard about their house in Yorkshire, their fraudulent insurance claims for storm damage, and listened to the importance of each and every gadget they had brought with them, how much they cost and how they were shipped, (they had spent a year in Kenya and had made a list for future reference), we said that we would definitely love to see their manual washing machine the next time we came, and made a run for it.

Why on earth would anyone go to the bother of importing a manual washing machine? More to the point, how could a washing machine be manual?

The service at Juliette's bed and breakfast, without Mike's company, fell into a steep decline (quite a feat). Chicken broth with imaginary vegetables or fried rice with 'spices' that looked like weevils, were set before us with an astounding enthusiasm. Juliette stood over us, nodding and beaming, while we decided whether the food was safe to eat.

We looked forward to moving into our own accommodation and were pleased when the visit to an empty property was arranged. The house at Anse à la Mouche was beautiful. We got a lift there, and help with our luggage, up the short driveway between high, glossy bushes to a fairly modern construction, perched at the top of a rise, above the bay below. The thrill of entering our new home was electric. On the right, was a narrow kitchen with the usual equipment (but without washing machine!) and, further inside, a large lounge and dining room with modern, chunky, functional furniture and a wall-mounted television. None of this registered very much, though, as we both gazed out at the enormous balcony, which gave onto a jungle of trees and exotic vegetation swaying in the breeze blowing up from the sea.

"Bloody hell!" said Carol. "Windy buggering Bay!"

"Fart a dart! It's gorgeous!" I replied, already opening the glazed door and stepping into the moist afternoon air.

We both stood, leaning out over the low wall, gawping. If I'd filled my lungs any more, they'd have burst. Then, Carol sat in one of the chairs and put her feet on the coffee table. I turned, sat down on the wall and put back my head, still dizzy with delight. Above me, looking back, was a lizard. It flicked its tail and shot out its tongue, while I decided whether I minded living with reptiles. I'd done it before, at university, so I could do it again. (Poor joke, slightly predictable, sorry.)

"Beau Vallon, you can keep," murmured Carol.

"Hello, lizard," I said, wishing I had a tail to flick.

Carol looked up and smiled. It was perfect. A big, stretchy moment that would leave its impression on my young, absorbent mind forever.

There were two bedrooms at the side of the house, looking on to more jungle and, just visible, the side of our neighbours' house. It was an isolated spot without a mechanical sound to be heard. We would be on our own. Girls against the jungle.

I opened up my suitcase and stood before the built-in wardrobe stunned by the sight of a very large, brown, dead-looking spider.

"Carol!" I called. "Could you come here a second?"

"It's dead," she said.

"Sure?"

Carol sighed and made to pick it up. With an enormous jump, 'Legs' Lazarus proved us wrong. We both screamed and hoped that it would not run. It didn't. Perhaps it was half-dead. Eventually, Carol put a bowl over it and took it to the bottom of the driveway, while I fretted and hoped that it wasn't a homing spider.

"There! All right now, you lily-livered dunderhead?"

"Do you think it will come back?"

"Funny you should say that."

I knew that I would regret asking, but I couldn't stop myself. "Why?" *You know I don't like them. Don't mess about!*

"It's just that I had a pet spider for ages, when I was about ten."

"Really?"

"He made a web in my pants drawer, called him Gusset, Gus for short, and I fed him on dead flies from the window ledge."

"I didn't know you liked insects."

"They weren't for me, they were for Gus."

I put on my best cold stare. "What happened to it? Was it a big one?"

"Not to start with. But it grew quite a bit."

"All those flies?" I don't know why I said this. The presentiment that something more was on its way was almost unbearable.

"Yep."

"So…?" *Did I really want to know?*

"Oh, it just disappeared one day. Opened the drawer and it was gone."

I thought about a knicker-nesting spider on the loose, and shuddered.

"Yeah. Just vanished. Then, about a week later it was back."

"It came back?" I was too young for a hot flush, but I felt my whole body overheating.

"Yep. It was wearing a top hat and cloak. Waving a magic wand. Homing spider."

"I hate you!"

"I know you do."

There was a tussle, in which I felled Carol and she somehow got me in an arm lock. Neither of us was the kind of girl to give in, so we waited until we were both bored enough to stop.

Anyway, with all this talk of spiders, I became obsessed for a while. I noticed that there were webs between all the telegraph wires, large ones. Apparently, these belonged to bird-eating spiders! Could it be that we had come to a horror film set and would be secretly observed, as giant arachnids worked to cocoon us and suck us dry while we slept? I unpacked, warily, looking out for peripheral movement, but all was well and soon, my terror put aside, I was relaxing on the balcony, sipping Seybrew, in lieu of wine or something stronger.

"Cheers!" said Carol.

"To us!" I replied, leaning back and checking on our lizard, who was checking on us.

"Where can we get a pizza round here?" asked Carol.

"Ah. Might be a problem. Have to make do with Spanish omelette tonight. Hungry now?"

"I'll chop the onions."

"Ah…"

To the Island

The coach came at 6.30am, as promised. We had slept well and risen early to eat cereals with orange juice (instead of milk), marvelling at the small insects that had floated to the top and wondering whether to consume them or not. I fished out most of mine; Carol said it was a waste of protein. We walked down the driveway, breaking the skeins of silk our friendly eight-legged cohabitors had spun during the night, came to the road and watched as the sky brightened suddenly in an equatorial sunrise that resembled a magic trick on an epic scale.

"What time is it?" asked Carol. "I wonder if buses are on time here."

Just then, a coach veered round the corner, its driver clinging on to the steering wheel, and climbed the hill towards us, barely slowing for the bend and carrying on without stopping.

"Hey!" we shouted. "Wait!" We ran after it a little, but to no avail.

"Is there a phone in the house?" said Carol, when we had walked back, disappointed and worried in equal parts.

"There is, but it's not connected."

"Shit! Why didn't he stop?"

"Dunno."

Eventually, we walked down the hill to a shack that sold general supplies and somehow the man behind the counter got a message through to the authorities and a car was sent to pick us up.

The driver smiled a lot and spoke very little. The coastal road was winding and I was reminded of a fairground ride I'd been on with my mother in Blackpool called The Mousetrap.

"Slow down a bit, mate," said Carol, leaning forward and tapping our driver on the shoulder.

This made things worse. Smiling broadly, we were treated to an enthusiastic monologue that seemed to be mainly about his brother, and involved fish of enormous proportions. He laughed, nodded and rolled his eyes in the mirror while Carol and I dug our fingernails into the back of each other's hands and sweated. By the time we arrived, I had become quite rigid and, if it hadn't been for Carol, would have stayed in the world I had created for myself, where cars were made of cotton wool and could fly.

The boat had waited. It wasn't like any other boat I'd ever seen before, except in old war films, but by this time, I would not have been surprised if it had been fashioned from a large sea creature or a cunningly hollowed out giant banana.

"Isn't this a landing craft?" I muttered.

"As long as it floats, I don't care what you call it," replied Carol.

Dick and Penny were there, amongst others.

"What kept you?" asked Penny, grinning like an old hand.

"Coach didn't stop," I said, bowing a little to the other passengers, by way of apology.

There was a general murmur of unsurprised acknowledgement and a couple of comments suggesting that the notification of bus drivers about newly recruited teachers was not always successful. We stepped up and over onto a bench, delivering ourselves into whatever future lay before us. I noticed the pungent smell of the engine and wondered whether I'd packed my Ventolin.

"Bloody Nora! Is that it?" Carol looked out across the Indian Ocean towards our place of work, a tiny island in the middle of an enormous mass of open water.

The captain, who resembled our driver so much that I finally realised it was our driver, flashed us a Jack Nicholson smile and let out the throttle. We sat back to enjoy the ride, trying to ignore the acrid black smoke that blew back into the boat. At least we couldn't plummet into the sea on a steep bend; sinking would be an altogether more leisurely experience.

The crossing was calm and pleasant, apart from the nauseating smell, and there was an exquisite air of anticipation on board. Small smiles were sent out and we reminded each other of names and subjects we would teach, asking about such trivia that serve to pad out superficial conversation. Apart from Dick and Penny, there was Harald, Jocelyn, Rose, Cedric, Marc and Emily. This was not the only boat that delivered teachers to the island.

We chugged along, pushing against currents that were, it was rumoured, treacherous and infested with sharks. We listened to Marc telling us about a group of inebriated tourists who had tried to swim from one island to another and had lost three members of their group en route. I shuddered and Carol yawned.

The captain wore his quiet grin as jauntily as his over-sized cap, barely looking where he was going, and I scanned the boat for life jackets or saftey instructions. Drowning, explosion or shark? I couldn't decide which I would prefer.

"Last term, the engine blew up and we drifted for a couple of hours. No radio. Luckily they found us before we were swallowed up by the Indian Ocean," mused Jocelyn.

Having since seen various sensationalist films in the 'group of people lost in the middle of the ocean waiting to die' genre, I now realise that the danger of disappearing forever, an undetectable blip on the watery landscape, was not only real, but had already almost come to pass on several occasions.

Of course, nothing happened this time. We made it across and jumped down into the shallows, as the ramp was lowered not quite near enough to the shore to avoid us getting our feet wet. We were escorted to our respective schools – there were two on the island and, to my initial horror, Carol would not be in the same one as me. I soon realised, however, that it might be a good thing – we didn't want to be in each other's pockets all the time and, besides, it would make for more interesting conversation at the end of the day. I followed our small group, as Carol and the others boarded a bus to take them to the second school on the other side of the island.

The sky was a holiday-brochure blue and the breeze from the ocean was strong enough to disturb the cloth of the dress I was wearing. It was pleasant to be aware of the contours of my body beneath my clothes and I examined my fellow teachers, disappointed to see that there would be no one to share them with (contours, not clothes).

I remember the staff room, but in no great detail. In many ways, it was the same as any other I had seen over the years. Functional, and filled with disparate furniture and suspicious glances. This time, we were housed in a small quadrangle of wooden buildings, one of which was the headmaster's office. He was a diminutive, energetic, but quietly spoken man with a full head of very dark hair and expensive-looking spectacles. We saw him rarely, and it was easy to forget that he existed, until cryptic messages appeared in our pigeon holes or on the huge, festooned notice board.

Many of the teachers came from Mauritius and Sri Lanka. There was a colourful combination of character and dress; amongst them, women in saris who'd brought along their knitting, brooding men in cotton shirts and trousers, who sat apart and looked important, and the odd European, who seemed only partially integrated yet vaguely and a little awkwardly superior. I quickly became aware that, even in this staff room, there would be a pecking order. One that would be essential to work out.

Dick and Penny had gone off with Carol to the other school and so I was left for a while, marginalised and sulking, although distracted to some extent by the imminent arrival of my first lesson. As far as I can remember, there were no books for the students, but a photocopier was available on site, with a limited selection of textbooks produced by publishers I'd never heard of, or whose ideas had been superseded ten years previously. I was glad that one of the boxes I'd packed was full of teaching materials I'd used in Greece. The students here would not be the same, but the worksheets could be adapted.

And so, with pedagogical strategies forming between my ears like fractals, and with minutes to spare, I took my small bag of tricks and headed outside to find my classroom, my heart full of trepidation as I trod a path that was unfamiliar to me, noting that, amongst the trees, there were constructions, open on two sides and set in groups of four, with corrugated-metal sloping roofs. The classrooms. In each of these buildings, there were large numbers of desks, chairs and even larger numbers of untidily distributed, uniformed students, some of whom appeared to be asleep and others who watched me pass by with expressions surprisingly devoid of curiosity. If someone had told me that there had been an invasion of the Body Snatchers at breakfast, I would not have raised an eyebrow. At first, such blatant lethargy would be a challenge, but I felt I was not only up to it, I was hungry for my new career, warts and all, to meet me head on.

"Good morning!" I cried, smiling for England. "Hello!" I waved, working the crowd into a frenzy of mild indifference. The blood raced round my body, feeding my super-charged brain, to no avail. I was primed for action, my fuse lit, but the audience looked right through me.

A girl's face lit up for a moment and then resumed its dull stare, another looked out at me as though through a clearing mist, and then away. One by one, the girls cast their brief glances in my direction, just as a cow might look up at a passing walker, with little interest.

I realised, using my honed analytical powers, that they were not as excited to see me as I was to see them, but I was confident I could change all that with my sparkling personality and avant garde teaching methods. They were mine to mould. How could they not be inspired?

It struck me all at once that they were girls, every single one of them. The other school must be for the boys! It was a simple arrangement and one that I felt I should have surmised earlier. Only later would I realise the full importance of such segregation.

Darkness and Light

The teaching days were long and hot. Long, because the timetable was British and hot because of the tropical sun, which beat down relentlessly on the corrugated roofs. I needed all my wits about me to make sure that, by the end of the lesson, I had managed to interest at least some of my students enough to keep them awake.

I learned all their names by the end of my first week, but was disconcerted when, by simply changing a hairstyle or moving to a different position in class, they all became unrecognisable. I made frequent mistakes. If I'd been worried about credibility, I'd have been in trouble. Fortunately, it was obvious that I had been accepted for the birdbrain that I was. Some of the girls listened to me and some of them tried the exercises I put before them, curious about the new methods and learning quickly that a more liberal approach inevitably meant less for them to do. If they decided to make an effort, they would make their teacher happy, if they decided to play dead, their teacher would redouble her efforts to engage them. They were in a win-win situation. I foolishly persevered, believing that they liked me and would therefore eventually come around and produce their best work.

"You have to do it their way," said Carol.

"Which is?"

"Chalk and talk."

"Is that what you do?"

"More or less. It's all very well doing role play and phonetic stations, but in the end, it'll get you into trouble."

I didn't understand. And, what was more important, I had never heard of 'phonetic stations'. So Carol explained the game to me, as she had heard it played in the classroom adjoining her own, and I decided to use it in my next lesson.

"Fancy going out tonight?" she asked.

"Where did you have in mind?"

"Just down the hill. There's a bar, apparently."

This was news to me. "All right."

'Just down the hill' turned out to be an hour's walk, or rather, stumble. There was no moon and it was pitch black outside. We came upon the local store, its sign reflecting a dim light, either coming from the interior of the shop or from the background radiation left over after the Big Bang. Either way, it was a welcome sight. We knew the road, but in the dark, the place seemed like a different planet, where invisible trees rustled menacingly and the squeaks of low flying bats made us jumpy. Little did these hapless rodents know that the locals would soon have some sport knocking them down from their leafy hideouts and make them into bat curry. (This is a true fact and not something I have made up for your entertainment…)

"Shall we go back?" I suggested.

"Nearly there, now," Carol lied.

We passed by a number of fluorescent smiles: men, their bodies obscured by the darkness, baring their teeth at the side of the road, presumably drunk on the cheap South African sherry supplied by the shop we had passed earlier. I supposed that, if there were no cat's eyes to guide us, then we should be grateful for this local alternative.

"Listen," said Carol.

I listened. "Can't hear a thing," I replied.

"Great, isn't it?" It was just possible to make out the soft glow of gentle euphoria on my lovely pal's face.

We walked on in silence and awe, each imagining our own place in this new world. I pictured the islands, protruding from the surface of the Indian Ocean, blips on a radar, just high enough above sea level for life to thrive and grow, for schools to be built and teachers to be imported and housed, for children to be educated and grow up with a more cosmopolitan view of the wider world. I sensed the shadow in the night that was Carol and wanted to hug her, secure in the knowledge that she shared my magnanimity and passion. Measuring the empathy of two beautiful minds floating in the night.

"I hope there isn't ever a tsunami," said Carol. "Cos, if is there ever was, we'd be fucked!"

I was pulled out of my quiet reverie with a jolt. It was an uncomfortable observation, mainly because it was irrefutable.

Eventually, as we followed the coastal road, wondering why we had believed anything that Marc had said, we rounded a bend and saw lights. It wasn't a bar, it was an sprawling hotel, low-lying and luxurious, off our school route and therefore new to us.

"This'll do," said Carol, linking arms with me and steering me under the enormous sign, towards the sound of music, already dancing and ready for some fun.

"How are we going to get back?" I pestered, momentarily aware of practicalities.

"Don't worry about that. Marc can give us a lift, later."

Inside the hotel, there was a large, open-plan lounge with huge glass doors pulled back, beyond which, there was a terrace looking out onto a glittering swimming pool and, further on, the glint and flash of the ocean. In the corner of the lounge, half on and half off a low stage, discoloured with use and badly put together, there teetered the band. Four men, impressively relaxed, both in demeanour and the keeping of a rhythm I had not previously encountered. I felt as though I had crept into the gap between two universes, where there was dissonance and chaos, the brute and the sophisticated uneasily married. I needed a point of reference.

When I found one, it was as though I had come up for air after an investigatory dive. I broke the surface into a world that I recognised, relieved and invigorated, my pulse alive to the potential for fun. Outside, on the terrace, was Marc, with a group of people we had not met before. People of our own age, wanting to rip it up on a Friday night.

"Bev! Carol! You found us!" Marc rose and, laughing irresistibly, came to gather us lovingly into the fold.

"This is Marianne, Thierry, Emile, Sonia, Astrid and Rosa."

They all smiled, as I nodded, forgetting their names instantly, noting that there were four girls and two rather plain-looking men. We sat and Marc ordered drinks, as the band started another song, this time with vocals.

"Oh, there's Sven! Hey! Over here! Sven!"

Carol and I looked behind us and then at each other. Carol winked and I swooned. The eye-candy had arrived at last!

It was always a surprise to me when I met someone that I was instantly attracted to. Sven made my stomach somersault and my brain buzz. He sat opposite and looked as though he might spontaneously combust with the heat of his own gorgeousness.

Carol gave me one of her looks that I had come to dread. She would 'fix me up' it said. I wanted to hide. I begged her not to do anything, with my 'please don't do anything' look. But it was too late.

"Sven – is that Danish?"

Sven, obviously used to such enquiries, let loose a twinkle and a grin that would kill at twenty paces. "It's Swedish," he said.

He can speak! I thought.

"We're English," said Carol.

"I guessed," replied Sven, laughing now.

"Are you out here on your own?" Carol fixed him with a plucky smoulder, and I watched his perfect features conspire to form a film star smile, wide, bright and utterly beguiling. I had just taken a mouthful of Piña Colada. Swallowing would be almost impossible.

"He's with me, actually," said the girl called Marianne, taking his hand, and looking exquisite.

Shit! Shitty shit, shit!

"That's a shame!" mused Carol, undeterred. "We were hoping he might be the answer to our prayers."

"What prayers are those?" asked Sven, obviously curious, and ignoring Marianne for the moment.

Carol had gone too far already, but I knew there would be more to come. Marianne looked as though she would like to kill us.

"We're looking for someone to give us blond babies."

Sven's laugh was explosive. Marianne scowled and then smiled broadly, catching on that the conversation was ironic, that Carol was harmless. British humour! Hilarious!

While they laughed and pointed, pointed and laughed, I caught Sven's eye and saw the element of doubt that would keep me going. My hussy tendencies were on red alert. My pal Carol had paved the way. All I had to do was to get rid of Marianne, who, I had decided, must be no more that a casual fling.

The band played on and on, running out of melodies so that the imperfect yet infectious tunes seemed to be on a crazy loop, making us dance more elaborately and applaud more loudly. The cocktails were strong, and the atmosphere of the bar moulded to the will of its paying guests, luring us to spend more time, more money. We were akin to insects attracted to a neon sign, happy to swoop and batter ourselves to pieces, wondering at the pleasure to be had on an island a thousand miles from anywhere, where the band, the bartenders and the waiters saw to our every need with a level of benign disaffection that I had only come across in my third year classes when I had taught in Milton Keynes.

Marianne was wary. She guarded Sven well that night. Marc told us on the way home that it was not serious between them, but that Marianne was intent on marriage. Sven was a free spirit. They had been together for almost a year, but in that time, Sven had strayed several times with local girls and with colleagues.

"It will not be difficult to get him," he said, casting a glance in my direction. "If that is what you want."

He should be so lucky! I thought, delightedly.

Centipede vs. Broom

The first weeks went by. My classes were exhausting. A British timetable was most definitely unsuited to the tropics. It didn't work on so many levels that it was difficult not to sympathise with the almost total apathy by the end of the day, due to extreme fatigue, of the girls I was trying to teach.

The classrooms were basic, and open to the air on two sides, which was all well and good, however the metal roof soon heated up and caused the temperature to rise anyway. Desks were in short supply, as were chairs, so each morning was a scramble to grab a place to sit. Once installed, there were no books. We relied on photocopies, which had to be organised well in advance – not one of my strong points. I don't know whether the students had pens and pencils, but if they did, they generally didn't bring them to class, so I took to taking a collection with me each day. The provision of writing implements alone was setting me back a tidy sum. There was no audio-visual equipment, obviously; so making lessons interesting was down to the teacher. I did my best.

I should explain that Ste. Anne was not just a school; it was a way of life. Before coming to their first class at 9.00am the girls had prepared lunch and set tables for the hundreds of students and teachers at the school. They lived on the island during term time, without the provision of services of any kind and had a whole host of duties to perform, taking on the various chores in turn. on a rota basis. They were allowed one hour of television after they had done their homework and eaten dinner, again, prepared by the *responsab* for that particular duty.

They were supervised by *animateurs*, who were generally disliked for their brusque manners and spot checks. The girls' bags and rooms were routinely searched, which they took exception to, as most people would. I have no idea what they would be hiding, but I suppose young people always find a way to have something illegal about their person.

In short, my students were knackered and disgruntled before they arrived, and asleep well before the end of the school day.

At first, my classroom experience was a trial by fire, especially for a young(ish!) teacher like me, who wanted to put her heart and soul into each and every lesson. However, the girls were innately cheerful, if lacking in conscientiousness, and I gradually worked out how to teach them something. I had to slow down and they had to speed up. Hopefully, we would meet somewhere in the middle.

During an early attempt at teaching them to use adverbs correctly, and just as Marisa, my most enthusiastic student, had fallen asleep, making the flat-out-on-the- desk headcount five, a cry went out and several students jumped up, shouting and gesticulating to each other. It was difficult not to be pleased at such a high level of activity and my initial thoughts were of gratitude towards whatever or whoever it was that had injected such excitement into the lesson.

"Miss! Miss! Centipede!" they shouted.

I saw my chance to do some real teaching.

"Okay. Sit down *quietly* and tell me *slowly* and *calmly*, what is the matter. Notice how I use adverbs to describe actions," I said, smiling pedagogically.

"No. No, Miss! Get away! Centipede!" they repeated, still dancing around.

I thought they were overreacting. After all, what harm could a centipede do to anyone? I looked up to the rafters and, at first, could see nothing out of the ordinary.

"There, there! Be careful, Miss!" They moved further back.

"All right. I can't see anything…" It occurred to me that they might be winding me up to distract me, exactly as my peers and I had done at school in England on countless occasions when we were young and easily amused by such tomfoolery.

Just as I was going to re-focus the lesson, and reinforce the importance of adverbs and word order with another pertinent and entertaining example, there was a fairly noticeable *slap*, as something very large dropped from the roof and landed at my feet, wriggling and taking off at great speed. It was around the length and width of a twelve-inch ruler, with a ridiculous number of pumping legs.

The cries of the students became shrill, disturbing the lesson next door so that faces appeared round the corner and the mayhem began to spread. The girls darted this way and that, none of them brave enough to stamp on the centipede, which was, I had to admit, unlike any I'd ever seen before.

"Get the broom!" said the Mauritian teacher from the class next door. "Quickly!"

"Did you notice the adverb, girls?" I commented, brightly.

My colleague smiled thinly, put her knitting down on a convenient desk and grabbed the broom, which had arrived in the nick of time, as the dratted insect was about to escape the shifting yet fairly effective barrier of schoolgirls' legs. Raising the large wooden classroom accessory over her head and bringing it down onto the offending centipede with a thwack, the teacher stunned the beast and assumed a Bruce Willis stance, as the children cheered and clapped, finishing off the unlucky invader and kicking its twisted lifeless body away into the undergrowth. It was difficult not to be just a little appalled.

The knitting, the broom and the heroic, sari'd rescuer disappeared, after which, things returned more or less to normal.

"Why were you so afraid of a harmless centipede?" I asked, when they had settled and were writing down some sentences from the board.

"Because its bite is poisonous, Miss," they confided earnestly, eyes wide, heads nodding.

Later, when I was recounting the entertaining tale to my new friend Rose, who also came from Mauritius, I got the same kind of reaction.

"You should be careful, you know. They are dangerous. If they bite you, you have to go to hospital. The bite is very painful and can kill if not treated."

"Kill?"

"Yes, kill!" Rose looked like a horror film voodoo doll come to life. It would not be the last exaggerated warning I would receive on the island of Ste. Anne, where superstition and folklore held sway, and where it was commonly believed that to get your feet wet would result in a ten-day fever which would require total bed rest and a great many hours of teacher substitution in the classroom.

"Bunkum!" said Carol, when I told her that evening about my brush with death.

She was right, of course. Almost certainly.

Miriam

When we had arrived at Anse à la Mouche there had been a lot of sorting out to do, as you can imagine. Electricity bill deposits were a new concept for me, but relatively simple to sort out, involving a one-off payment, refundable when we left, as long as all bills had been settled in full. Phone contracts had to be set up. Also, we were paid in sterling, so we would have to exchange money regularly in Victoria - this was just a matter of remembering to do so, before we were down to our last rupee. Carol had a much better memory than I did, so that was okay – I would leave our day-to-day solvency to her.

What we weren't expecting at all was the queue of women outside our door on one of the first Saturdays after we moved in.

"Wakey, wakey! We've got trouble." Carol was wearing her bright pink, silky dressing gown with a dragon motif on the back.

"Eh? What time is it? What day is it?" I had a horrible thought that we had forgotten to get up and missed the bus to work.

"Saturday. Nine o'clock. God knows how long they've been out there."

"Who?" It was all too much. "Where?"

"Stick something on and come and have a look."

I put on my wrap-round leopard skin robe and went with Carol to the front door.

"Who's outside?" I whispered, pushing back the haystack that had replaced my hair during the night.

"Lots of women," she replied.

I listened to the babble of conversation and scowled, analysing the mood of the crowd, trying not to panic.

"Look!" said Carol, suddenly, and to be honest, alarmingly opening the door wide so that we could see outside and whoever was outside could see inside. I gasped. Women in multi-coloured dress. Lots of them.

Their chatter subsided for a second and then redoubled in volume as Carol slammed the door shut again.

"What the…?"

"No idea, my lovely tart."

"What shall we do? Do you think they're dangerous?"

Carol gave me one of her looks, and disappeared into her room.

"Get dressed!" she shouted.

There was a knock at the door.

"Quickly!" she added. "Before the crowd turns nasty and breaks down the door!"

By this time, I had seen the funny side, and was hopping around the bedroom trying to get my trousers on, barely suppressing my giggles.

"Perhaps they think we're famous," I shouted. "Bananarama girls. Kim Wilde. Come to get our autographs." It was possible!

Carol was ready in seconds, wearing one of her full-length, weekend kaftans. She agreed that my supposition was not beyond the realms.

"Know any songs?" I asked.

"Come on. Let's see what they want."

Requests? I wasn't sure I was ready for requests. I knew just about everything by Abba, so I crossed my fingers and stood behind Carol as she opened up.

What they wanted, all twenty-five of them, was to clean for us. They were under the impression that we would need their services and could afford to pay for them. It was an easy decision: The redistribution of wealth and the prospect of escaping doing our own housework – what could be more perfect?

Not being used to interviews from the other side of the desk, so to speak, we invited the first woman in and offered her a cup of tea, which she declined. She didn't want a beer, either.

"Good morning. My name is Carol and this is Bev," said Carol, beginning again from the beginning, after we were seated at the dining room table

We shook hands, awkwardly.

"I am Miriam. I can clean and tidy very well. My work is excellent."

Miriam was a fairly bulky woman of around twenty-five, who grinned a lot and didn't seem to be at all nervous.

I coughed. Then I asked, "Why do you want to work for us?" After all, this was the key question in any interview situation. Carol was unimpressed and sighed heavily.

"I need a job to pay for my abortion," replied Miriam, as quick as a shot.

It wasn't exactly the kind of answer I had expected. Even Carol was a little taken aback.

Miriam's smile widened as she took our surprise for interest, going on to explain that she had already had six and this would be her seventh. Before we could say this was really none of our business, she dived in deeper, explaining that there was a woman in the local community where she lived, who had very reasonable rates and a good safety record.

"There has only been one death. One out of many. Many!" Miriam communicated her awe and respect for such statistical excellence.

There was a momentary lull in the conversation while Carol and I cast about for something to say. I was wondering why Mike hadn't imparted this essential social bombshell during our very frank and comprehensive drunken discussion at Juliette's B & B. I was horrified by, and at the same time, sympathetic to Miriam's plight.

"When can you start?" I asked, at last.

"Today," replied Miriam.

We had a cleaner. We were contributing to the economic stability of the local area. Doing our bit to spread the love and the rupees. Of course, the ladies in the queue didn't see it that way and I was sorry that I couldn't summon a good strong wind to blow them all away, just as Mary Poppins had done.

Miriam said she would come three times a week during the mornings and tucked our spare key inside her bag. The following Monday, she set about dusting, scrubbing and polishing every surface so that when we came home after work the house shone and smelled fresh. By the end of the first week, she had broken a large bathroom mirror, dropped Carol's cassette player and stuck a knife into the freezer's electrics whilst trying to defrost it without turning it off.

"Very sorry," said Miriam.

"Doesn't matter," we chimed, sweetly.

The crunch came when, during the third week, the house being so clean that there was probably nothing to keep her occupied, Miriam decided to wash our clothes. There was no washing machine, as I have already mentioned, so we had been doing a hand wash and hanging stuff out to dry on the balcony. It seemed to work well. This, however, was not the Seychellois way.

The sight that met our eyes as we climbed the short rise to our house, happy to be home after a long day of teaching, will stay in my mind forever. There were most of our clothes, looking as though they had been tie-dyed and/or bleached, then pronged out to dry on the very large, very prickly bush just outside our front door.

"Christ on a bike! What's the silly tart done to our bloody clothes?"

I was speechless. In fact, I think I went into shock as I realised that the washed-out rags I could see dangling in the sun were my treasured tee shirts, shorts and dresses. It was too much to take in.

Carol dropped her bag and tried to detach a once checked shirt that now sported a selection of pink clouds on its front and lots of small holes around the bottom.

"Bloody Nora! She's shredded our stuff."

"Not my red dress!" I couldn't believe it. My red Top Shop strapless mini was now a dusky pink shapeless rag. "It's dry clean only!" I whimpered.

We got the clothes down and salvaged what we could, which wasn't much. We were casual dressers, but not that casual!

"What shall we do?" said Carol, showing her more serious side for once.

"We could get some dye and a pack of needles and cotton," I replied. But my heart wasn't in it.

"No! What shall we do about Miriam?"

We both knew that Miriam had to go. Carol offered to do the dirty deed when she didn't turn up on the next cleaning day. News had obviously travelled fast. So, one afternoon, Carol bravely set off to find her, with a month's wages (which didn't amount to very much) stuffed into an envelope.

We would have to break our own mirrors and ruin our own clothes from now on.

No Need to Queue

The following weekend, we got the bus into Victoria, the capital of Mahé, which, together with the other one hundred and fifty-five islands, was part of the Seychelles group. The largest of the islands, Mahé is only twenty-nine kilometres long, so going places didn't take too long, despite the winding roads. The regular bus stopped at the bottom of the hill where our house was set, although, in the heat, it was not pleasant to walk far without shade. We were not yet used to the constant mugginess either, which brought with it a level of saturation that made the clothes from our now limited wardrobe damp, and would eventually rot our shoes.

The lush scenery on either side of the almost unfrequented road, oozed out at us, and it was easy to imagine the vast and intricate habitats, in the cool dark shadows, of an array of animal and insect life, most of which would be new to us and some of which was unique to individual islands. We stayed on the road.

Halfway down the hill, the local shop was doing a roaring trade in cheap alcohol and, already, there was a small group of men enjoying life in the slow lane, while the women went out to work and gave birth to their babies.

"Did you say there's no marriage here?" asked Carol, as we continued past the men with ecstatic smiles.

"Mostly," I replied. "The men attach themselves to more than one woman and the result is a bit messy. But there are marriages. Probably for the people who can afford the service and the reception."

"Sounds grim," said Carol.

I agreed completely, Miriam's stark views still clear in my thoughts. "I suppose it's quite natural here."

"You think? Isn't it just evolution? Wonder how many years it'll be before emancipation hits the Seychelles."

I was wary of making pronouncements on a culture I had little knowledge of, but it was hard not to believe that ignorance (or rejection) of birth-control methods, coupled with the practice of co-habitation on a grand scale, might mean that things would not change quickly.

"If they had a better television station, they wouldn't have so many kids," announced Carol, her pragmatic self to the fore.

It was true that we had only found programmes that seemed to be channels for government propaganda, and endless local news. Each morning, there would be a role call of people who were requested to come back to work; their return was presumably unlikely as, as far as we knew, there were no sanctions, in fact we had been surprised to read in the first paragraph of our employment contract that employees of the National Youth Service were entitled to no more than sixty days' sick pay per annum. In the land of folklore, this was apparently scant comfort.

We reached the bus stop, narrowly avoiding being run over by a mad driver in his Mini Moke, on the wrong side of the road. In the Seychelles, you drive on the left.

"Dozy bastard nearly had us!" Carol gesticulated and fumed.

We settled a little away from the road to wait for the bus, and contemplated the horizon. The view from the road was surreal, when you remembered that the blue ocean that stretched out before us continued uninterrupted for a thousand miles in every direction. The nearest substantial land mass was the neighbouring island of Mauritius and the nearest continent was Africa. We intended to make the most of our stay, and visit as many places as we could in the holidays. Little did we know at the time that we were to be bound by strict rules on travel. But more of that later.

The bus arrived, more or less full. There were a few seats left so we grabbed two and observed our fellow passengers quietly. The mix of race was striking. There were beautiful, fine featured young women, with long dark hair, perfect skin and regular features, almost but not quite Chinese in appearance. I was reminded of the Girl from Ipanema and wondered what one particularly gorgeous girl thought of our *PolyBlonde* hair and ruddy complexions. Other women were of obvious African descent, wearing voluminous gathered skirts and vast floral blouses. They had short, wiry hair, often pinned back, muscular arms and round faces. Miriam had been of African stock. I hoped she would find another job, but I doubted she would be able to keep it for long.

Carol and I were the only Westerners on board, but, apart from a casual glance now and then, we did not attract much attention. Just mildly adventurous, fairly scrawny tourists - the type that could not afford car hire. It was as though people lived in a trance, whether due to the climate, or the political system, which did not seem to reward initiative or competition and, as we would find out later, did not criticise incompetence.

The roads on Mahé were, at that time, either new or fairly well maintained, and serious potholes were few. The speed at which the national bus took the bends was a fraction of that of our National Youth Service driver in his superior luxury coach; there was, nevertheless, enough of a drop to make the journey sobering. It became apparent that, although there was a maximum load clearly stated on a plaque at the front of the bus, this was given no consideration. The aisle filled up and then filled up some more, until the bus resembled a London Underground carriage at rush hour. We sweltered and hoped that, eventually, people would start getting off.

"Egads! We have to get some transport, my beautiful dullard. I don't fancy squeezing into one of those with our shopping on the way back."

I supposed Carol was right. If we wanted to see the rest of the island in comfort we would have to get a car. But for now, we were out to shop, with an eye to replacing some of our ruined clothes, picking up some drinks and something other than lentils or rice for dinner.

The market was in full swing. Exotic fruit and vegetables gently warmed under the tarpaulins. We bought breadfruit (not yet aware that they grew on trees only a few metres from our house), green bananas, mangoes and paw paw. There wasn't a lettuce or a Granny Smith's apple in sight. At the fish stall, there was such bounty as to be frightening. Never had I seen such enormous fish, fresh from the bright, unpolluted waters of the Indian Ocean. Even so, the variety was limited, as we had arrived too late in the day to experience the full range of produce. Most of the cheaper options had disappeared. We bought *wahoo*, a fish with vertical blue stripes and a greenish back. It was relatively expensive but highly recommended as good eating.

"Are you any good at cooking fish?" Carol asked.

"I can cook cod or haddock. Even halibut, in the oven with a little milk, butter and nutmeg." The list was short, but I was confident I could manage.

"Good. Don't like touching it. Don't mind eating it."

I slid the package into our rucksack and we perused the vegetable stalls again, experimenting a little with some of the chilli peppers on display, as well as purchasing aubergines and tomatoes, garlic and ginger, coriander, fenugreek, cumin, and cloves.

"We're going to need a bigger bag next time," said Carol.

"Want me to take a turn?"

"You can have it on the bus."

We were nearly done with food shopping, but decided to go in search of the 'western' supermarket we had been told about by the French expats, who were paid a lot more than we were and weren't afraid to rub our noses in it. So, when we did find it and realised that we could afford hardly anything in it, we began to feel more than a little put out.

"Bugger! I really fancy some salad, but this manky-looking lettuce is nearly two quid," said Carol.

"None of it looks fresh. I suppose it must be imported from South Africa. Have it if you want it. Let's live a little!"

After further investigation, Carol decided that the lettuce was on its last legs and probably wouldn't survive the journey home, so we found some oranges that looked edible and bought a couple of those instead.

The wine section was also well beyond our means and so we snuck out with the oranges, a couple of lemons and some unconvincing cheddar cheese, which cost nearly as much as all the shopping we had got from the market.

"This is depressing," observed Carol.

"Come on, let's look in some clothes shops."

"What are you expecting? Top Shop? Chelsea Girl?"

As it turned out, Carol's cynicism was well founded. The fashion was for cotton dresses, beautifully made not to fit or suit people like us, and floral tops and skirts that would have made even Debbie Harry look old-fashioned. We considered sarongs, but decided that Miriam had spared enough of our clothes to avoid cross-culture dressing for the moment. We did find a couple of nice scarves for Carol and a host of decorations for our hair, which cheered us up no end.

I re-distributed our purchases, but the bags were still heavy and we didn't relish the trip back. The heat was wearing and the fish would not last long. We wanted to get home for lunch while it was still edible, followed by a bit of reading on the balcony.

"Finished?" asked Carol.

"Yeah. You?"

"Hours ago!"

The bus stop was deserted and we had high hopes of a more comfortable trip back. There was a man with more wrinkles than most octogenarians could hope to accumulate, sitting with his eyes closed, in the middle of the only bench in the only bit of shade around. There were ten minutes to wait.

As we checked our bags and talked about what we would do with the nicely warming fish, people sauntered up and formed small, menacing groups, until we thought we should get into some kind of queue in order not to be pushed to the back. We quietly asserted ourselves in a way so typical of the British, standing our ground, next to the person who had arrived before us, and in front of everyone else. The notion of a queue, however, tends to fall apart if only two people recognise it. We watched as women arrived with bags, chickens and babies, swarming in a most disorganised way and blocking off any clear passage forward. We were stuck.

When the bus did arrive, there was a surge, with plenty of pushing and shoving, a fair amount of good-natured shouting and much passing of things through the windows, including a newborn baby wrapped in a blanket.

"Come on! Otherwise we'll have to wait for the next one!"

"Maybe that would be better," I said, not relishing the intimate contact necessary for the chance of a seat.

But Carol was determined, elbowing her way through, both of us hanging onto the shopping bags and ignoring the rules of social behaviour we had lived by until then, we progressed to the entrance and paid.

We got seats in the middle, formerly occupied by a cage containing two bantams, which Carol removed and put in the aisle.

"I read somewhere that an airline that had double booked one of its planes in Sri Lanka decided that all the passengers should run three times around it to decide who got the seats."

"Maybe we should suggest it?"

"Maybe. But in the meantime, I think we should talk to Penny and Dick about where they got their Mini Moke."

"Have you got any cash?" I asked, remembering that Carol rarely had.

"I will have at the end of the month. I mean, how much can a crappy second-hand motor cost?"

Never make assumptions about anything in a foreign land...

Round the Bend

Rose was half my height, with short black hair shaped like a tea cosy, and had enough energy to power more than the twelve hour day required of us. I liked her immediately. She was a fantastic sneak and always passed on any tittle tattle, uncensored and unabridged, mainly relating to the other Mauritian teachers, mostly women, who didn't approve of ideas that challenged their own rather traditional views on teaching and just about everything else. They didn't care for me, it seemed.

The staff room was like any other I had been in, except that there were fewer chairs to sit on and a large table in the centre of the room around which this self-governing faction sat, pronouncing quiet judgements on just about everyone and everything, to the rhythm of knitting needles tick-ticking with a speed that I could never hope to achieve. (I was an excellent producer of extreme knitwear, notably a Starsky and Hutch cardigan which, when I was seventeen, was considered the height of fashion.)

Anyway, at one end of this table, there was a man, *sans* knitting, who always clasped his hands together and lowered his head a little, as if in prayer. Rose said that he had a stomach ulcer, two wives and seven children in Mauritius. He had elected himself chairman of the board and kept the sniping if not in check then certainly low key. Whenever Rose wanted to get gossip, she approached the head man first, then sat amongst the women, complimenting them on their clothes, hair or craftwork, before gently delving deeper to find out any interesting snippet of news.

I spent most of my free time with Rose. We sat together at lunch, picking through fish heads for a little meat and trying to intercept the cucumber salad before it disappeared. She told me about her hometown and said that her mother and father had paid for her education so that she could get off the island, get a well-paid job and send money back to Mauritius to help them.

"Do you have enough?" I asked.

"You're joking, right?" Her eyes were amazing when she stared, her irises floated free of the whites and moved from left to right minutely and at high speed. It was like watching a mini earthquake.

"No. Why would I be joking? We have trouble making ends meet, actually." It was true. We could not switch on the air-conditioning for fear of an enormous bill, we could not afford a lettuce or a bottle of decent wine.

"Really?" Her eyes vibrated anew. "The salary here is three times as much as I could earn in a school in Mauritius. Three times, at least."

"But that's not the point, Rose. The cost of living here means that we are poor."

"Ah! That is because you like the things that are imported. Local food and drink is very cheap or even free, if you go to the market at the end of the day. I can fill up my fridge for a week for only a few rupees."

"Canny!"

"What does 'canny' mean?"

"Clever."

Rose nodded. She obviously agreed with my assessment.

It was difficult to imagine where she had come from, despite her descriptions, and impossible to imagine the future she had in store for herself. I was humbled by the notion that she was helping to support her family, who, for their part, had made sacrifices for their daughter in order to give her the chance to train as a teacher. I admired their solidarity.

During one of our afternoon breaks, the level of noise in the staff room reached an elevated level and I wondered what was going on. Rose was instantly on hand to inform me that we would all be receiving an important memo in our pigeonholes before the day was out. It seemed that one of the headmaster's administrators was a bit of a snitch.

"What's it all about?"

She tapped the side of her nose and went over to the governing table, where she continued to be tolerated because of her nationality and the financial support she provided to her parents. She was a good girl, the women said. She knew what her duties were.

I looked through the lesson plan I had in mind for the last class of the day, unconcerned and only slightly curious about the impending memo, knowing that, even if we were all to be dismissed, I'd soon get over it.

I stood up to leave and Rose came with me, linking arms and grinning up at me with her usual shiny enthusiasm. "We have to take it in turns to clean the restrooms." Her choice of American syntax confused me for a moment.

"Restrooms?"

"The toilets. The female teachers have to draw up a rota. The students have complained that we should do more duties. They cook for us and wash the dishes. They have decided that we should clean our own toilets."

It was my turn to look amazed.

Before I could speak, Rose squeezed my hand and ran off to class. I strolled over to my block, seeing the campus in an entirely different light. This really was a different country, with an ethos that stretched the imagination of a girl from the Midlands who had been to Cambridge University and dined regularly at Queens' College. The idea of being a loo cleaner was absurd (I bridled with haughty indignation). I wondered what Carol would have to say.

At the end of the day, I approached our World War II ocean-going transport and, even from a distance, I could see that the group of teachers from the other school were more animated than usual. They must have had the same news. The fight was on, and things might get bloody.

"There's no way I'm cleaning bloody bogs!" It was my best friend in all the world.

"Scraping off other people's crap? No way, José!"

A plan of attack was being thrashed out and I listened as the conversation developed from a series of wild suggestions and sharp expletives to a more rational and reasonable approach.

"What we need is to protest, as a group," said Penny.

"Yeah. But we can't all go. We need a representative," said one of the others.

"Someone who's not going to back down. Someone who won't take no for an answer."

All eyes turned to Carol. I hoped they knew what they were doing.

"Nominations?"

"I nominate Carol."

"Second?"

"I second the nomination!"

"Carol? Will you be our representative?" asked Penny.

"Tell me what you want me to say, apart from *we're not cleaning the fucking toilets*, and I'll do it."

On the way back to Mahé, the details were discussed. What tone to take. How not to be threatening, or drive the headmaster into a corner. Whether we should turn up with banners, Marigolds and loo brushes. It didn't take long to hatch a plan, and Carol promised that it would be a cinch.

I wasn't sure it would be so easy.

Party Time!

It was almost the weekend. Nothing more had been said about loo cleaning and Carol was holding fire, in the hope that the management had seen the folly of its wild assumptions. Toiletgate could wait.

We ditched our somnolent students, feeling only slightly sorry that their weekend would be spent on the island under supervision, and would probably involve many hours of chores and homework. Still, we'd done our time as petulant teenagers, now we were fabulously talented grown ups, with money in our pockets and a bottle of Icebreaker (a brain-numbing South African white rum – reasonably priced) in the fridge.

We leapt onto the boat on Friday afternoon and were immediately informed by Anka, a woman who came from the then Yugoslavia and who was one of the most interesting people I would meet on the island, that she was having a party. She had a face that my overly romantic imagination told me had been hardened by the history of her country's struggles and a light that burned slowly in her eyes that said she feared nothing and no man. Also, it was rumoured that she threw great parties.

"Should be a good night. Make sure you bring wine. No wine, no entry!"

"Tell that to the Frenchies!" said Carol, yawning. "Tight buggers."

There was a general murmur of agreement. The ones we'd met had better jobs, better accommodation and obscene salaries (I remembered Rose's words), but so far, had been less than generous at social events.

"Are they coming?" I ventured. "Did you invite them?"

"Don't be ridiculous! They always find out about a party. Anyway, I wanted to invite Marc – he's a sweetie".

Anka was an easy-going person, most of the time. And, after all, the expatriate community was limited, with the long-stayers always eager for new blood. We were new and therefore both disproportionately desired and grateful when she invited us for the following evening's diversion.

Anka had lived on the island for more than ten years with her husband, Dragan and their daughter, Lou, who was seven, born in the Seychelles, and streetwise. They were marine biologists doing research into emerging species in the waters offshore. Dragan worked at this full-time and Anka did part-time teaching.

Anka made beautiful sketches of marine life, and Lou coloured them in. It was a deliciously irreverent way of recording data. She told us that the house was near the beach at Anse Boileau, up a steep road, against the backdrop of a mountain covered in trees so green and prolific that it was hard to believe they were real. It was clear that she had fallen in love with the Seychelles, and would stay on indefinitely.

We bagged a lift with Marc. It was only a few miles and probably walkable, but not in high heels and skimpy dresses, in the pitch darkness that descended at 6.00pm, so we clung on as the jeep rounded the corners, willing our driver to spend a little more time looking at the road and a little less at us. As usual, there was no light, apart from the headlights, so that it seemed as though we were flying, which was exhilarating and at the same time terrifying.

"Is this it?" I asked, as we drew up to a rather small and basic-looking house with several cars parked almost, but not quite off the road.

"This is it!" replied Marc, turning up the lecherousness of his smile and letting me see his oversized incisors glint in the moonlight.

"Come on! We don't want to miss the best bits," said Carol.

The evening was warm, the sky glowed with stars and the music was from the 80s. What more could we ask?

Anka was the perfect host, low-impact, hugely accommodating and ready with an opened bottle of red as she greeted us. The house was dark, apart from the kitchen, where too many people were gathered. We squeezed in and grinned at the guests we had yet to meet. Some of them grinned back, some scowled, some had been expats for too long.

"Don't bother about them. They're just jealous," whispered Carol.

Sven was there, looking ridiculously handsome. My pulse accelerated, despite my efforts not to be obvious or predictable.

"Drink?" he asked.

"Please," I replied, coolly trembling.

He didn't say I looked nice. He didn't have to.

"Where's Carol?" he asked, pouring wine and quietly smouldering.

I looked around. "Don't know. She always deserts me at parties."

"Are you …together?"

It wasn't the first time I'd been asked this question. "Most of the time," I replied, letting him work out for himself that I was more interested in men with blond hair, tanned skin and a Swedish accent than my lovely friend.

"How about you and Marianne?"

"Oh, most of the time," he said, handing me a glass.

We clinked.

Marianne hovered, letting us have a few more seconds and then whisked Sven away to attend to a catch on her bracelet.

I found Carol in the large living room, which had been cleared, the furniture pushed aside, making space for a dance floor. Carol was giving all she'd got to *Pop Music* one of our favourites from university days. Her dancing style had always been enthusiastic and tonight she looked as though someone had wound her up to maximum and set her spinning. I could see her lips moving to the lyrics and watched as people around her tried to emulate her jerking hips and writhing shoulders, all the time wary of her upper body movements.

We danced. It was what we needed. Anka joined us, so did Dragan. They introduced us to a few people and we had comical, half-heard conversations, nodding and smiling in what might have been the right places.

When I looked around, Carol had gone again, so I went out onto the balcony for some air. A large-bellied man holding a bottle of beer stood back to let me pass, a girl sat in one of the sun chairs looking either drunk or miserable, Anka was in a corner, snogging someone who wasn't her husband, and Sven was going down the steps into the unlit garden. I gulped down the rest of my wine, looked back inside the house for a moment, wondering where Carol had got to. Then, I followed Sven.

The night was humid and pungent with the heavy odour of vegetation, making the garden seem alive and yet dormant, which was a perfect description of how I felt, too. I shivered, partly from the cooling breeze on my damp forehead and partly because I couldn't see Sven and imagined him lurking somewhere close. Standing still for a moment, I listened to the movement of the trees, discernible over the music above. I felt as though I were being drawn deeper into something magical and strange. My breathing became faster and I knew what would happen. I knew I would not be able to resist.

Spiders (again) and Lizards

Sunday would be a day of rest.

"Tea?" Carol was up and wanted company.
"And toast?" I bleated.
"Nope. Bread's gone mouldy."
"Oh. What time is it?" I was being woken up against my will, on a Sunday morning, when the only bread in the house was inedible. For all I knew, Carol had no adequate reason for infringing my basic human right to a Sunday morning lie-in. It couldn't be more than eight o'clock in the morning. I wanted to go back to sleep. I made mumbling noises into my pillow.

"The time, my beloved trollop, is ten o'clock."

Somehow this weakened my defence. I turned over and looked up to see a small lizard and a large spider on the wall opposite. I was going to scream, but the lizard made sudden and short work of the eight-legged horror and I watched, delighted and repulsed at the same time.

"Coffee, please!" I didn't want to be forgotten.

I must have dozed off again. Carol called to say that breakfast was served on the balcony and I lumbered out, checking the walls and picturing the lizard/spider encounter I had witnessed in a semi-stupor, wondering whether I had dreamt it. Passing the mirror in the dining room, I saw that my hair had migrated to the left side of my head once more, and resembled the flame of a stylised Olympic torch.

There was no coffee so we had tea, made with powdered milk, and, in lieu of lovely crunchy buttery jammy toast there were healthy slices of ripe paw paw and juicy mango. Bummer.

"Thanks, my lovely culinary queen. I just saw a lizard eat a spider. It was gross."

Carol, unimpressed, let me settle in one of the sun chairs.

"Did it rain in the night?" I asked, sitting up and sniffing, looking out at the wet jungle and the blue, blue sky.

"Penny told me that we should put a bowl of water under each of the legs of our beds. Drowns them, apparently."

"Sounds gruesome." The bowl would have to be quite big. I imagined the morning harvest of soggy insects.

"There was a storm. Lots of thunder and lightning." Carol was eating biscuits, dunking them in her tea. I wanted some too. I decided that, as we were living in a Pinter play, I would continue the largely dislocated conversation.

"Have we got any?"

"Any what?"

"Bowls?"

Carol had her thinking face on. "Must have." Her expression brightened. "Good, last night. Ace music. Great to have a dance."

"Fab party. Can't remember the storm at all. Any more biscuits?"

"Just this one," she said, dunking it in her tea and inserting it whole into her mouth with an evil flourish. After a gratuitous smacking of the lips, she asked, "Do you remember telling Marc that he was the loveliest, funniest froggy you'd ever met?"

"No. And I would never say anything like that, even if I were drunk."

"Ha! Well, you can ask him on Monday. Where did you go off to, anyway?" Carol already knew. I could tell, despite her manufactured casualness.

"Tall, blond, gorgeous…" I pulled my legs up and hugged them.

"Yeah. Granted. But did you shag him?"

"Oh! How crude!"

"Bollocks! Tell me now, or I'll…Christ! Look at that lizard!"

There was another lizard chomping on an even larger spider, which was still trying to get away with the part of itself that hadn't yet been consumed.

"Bugger me! It must really have happened, unless it was a premonition. Bon appetit!" I said, pleased, but wondering how many other eight-legged horrors there might be in the house or under my chair, or on my head. "Better get those bowls sorted out for tonight. Ugh!"

"Well?"

"Well what?"

"Did you let him in?"

"Not quite. If it's any of your business!"

"Good girl! Keep him waiting. Best way."

"Did you see Marianne?" I asked, feeling pleased that Carol was proud of me.

"Oh, yes! She was looking for him. Lucky for you that Marc was primed, and told her he'd gone down the road to the beach. Think she's used to him disappearing. No need to feel guilty – she should ditch him. Not husband material."

"Easier said than done, though, eh?" I did feel a bit guilty.

Carol got up to get more tea.

"What did *you* get up to?" I called.

"Went down to the beach with Dragan."

I waited for her to come back, running through various scenarios. Perhaps this was the way it was. Expat society. Lots of desperate people sneaking off with each other at every opportunity. I remembered seeing Anka on the balcony, writhing against someone, unconcerned about doing so for all to see.

"Nothing happened. I do have *some* morals," said Carol, handing me an even less appetising cup of tea. "Sorry, had to re-use the teabags. Only a couple left."

I grunted. "So what did you and Dragan do, then?"

"Went for a walk. He took a huge flashlight and we climbed down onto the sand. So white and soft. Different to the Cornish beaches." Carol seemed to have lost track of what she was saying. This was unusual for her.

"So?" I prompted.

"So, we walked and he talked a lot about where he comes from. Told me about the inevitable break up of Yugoslavia and all the terrible things that have happened and will continue to happen. He thinks there'll be even bigger trouble there soon."

"Did you go for a swim?"

"Dragan said it was dangerous. The sharks come out to feed at night."

"Shit! Sharks? Doesn't the reef keep them out?"

"Apparently not. Don't know if there is one, anyway. Wrong type of island. He says there have been some serious casualties over the years and some deaths, too. The last one happened on the beach we were walking along."

"Really? Are you sure he wasn't just trying to impress you?"

"He's not going to get my knickers off by scaring me with shark stories. Anyway, I like him. That's all. Don't fancy him. *And*, he's married to Anka, for God's sake – why would he look at anyone like me?"

She had a point. "How long have you been with Dave, now? Must be ten years. Do you think he'll be faithful?"

"It was nine years when we broke up."

"You *what*?"

"We broke up. I didn't want to tell you."

"Fart a dart!"

"Anyway, I'm not looking for a replacement just yet," said Carol.

"Why didn't you say?"

"Because it's not sure. Who knows what's going to happen? We might end up together, we might not. In the meantime, we're free to do as we please. Satisfied?"

I said that anything she wanted to do was all right by me. Then I lay back and thought of Sven. I knew I had made an exceptionally bad choice, but at the time, I didn't care.

Principles and Politics

On our return to school the following Monday, the toilets had been cleaned, but not by us.

The headmaster called a meeting for the next day after lunch, and it was rumoured that he was fuming. It was not the done thing in a socialist republic to refuse to stick your hand down the u-bend just because it was unpleasant. If someone had to do it, then why not *you*?

I spoke to my colleagues and drew little response. The Mauritian knitting circle and their devout followers seemed to be ready to set aside their raglan masterpieces and take up the generously supplied Marigolds, happy to jostle the odd loo brush in the name of solidarity and in the hope of keeping their lucrative contracts. The handful European teachers were not keen on accompanying Carol and I on a visit to the headmaster's office to perform a pre-emptive strike, even though, they too, were against disinfecting the dunnies in their free periods. I had a feeling that, if the imminent staff meeting went ahead, the headmaster would find little or no opposition to his suggestion. It was imperative for someone to act and to act fast. We would have to see him before lunch!

I contacted Carol by note, sent with a runner, asking her to walk over during her free period so that we could put our case. Monsieur Albert was always in his office, so when Carol arrived, cursing about having to rush about at my beck and call, and complaining about a blister on her big toe, we knocked and he let us in, looking surprised and perhaps (we hoped), a little apprehensive.

We had the advantage of height until he told us to sit down, disarming us with a cheesy smile and the offer of a Fox's Glacier Mint.

"I hope you are enjoying your work with The National Youth Service. The children speak very highly of both of you. We value your commitment."

I recognised his tactics.

"We enjoy our teaching, Monsieur Albert. It's what we were contracted to do," said Carol, in a stroke of cunning so slickly delivered that I almost applauded.

"I see. Carol, isn't it?"

"It is."

"I presume then, that you have come to complain about the latest incentive to increase efficiency and create a just and reasonable working environment in which people share those responsibilities that may not be, shall we say, the choicest of tasks?"

I was too slow to interject, due to the clever strategy of the boiled sweet.

"Here in Seychelles we strive to be good citizens." He interlocked his fingers and sank back into his chair. "We believe that our people are equal, and that each one of us should be valued, respected, listened to."

"We are not cleaning the toilets, Monsieur Albert," said Carol.

I felt she had been too abrupt, too categorical.

"What Carol means to say, sir, is that we do not feel that we should undertake any duties that are not specifically mentioned in our contracts. For one thing, this would mean that we were being employed to do a job for which we hold no formal qualifications and for another, that we would be depriving a member of staff, who may have specialised in that particular field, of gainful and fair employment. If you refer to the political disruption during the miners' strikes under Margaret Thatcher, you will concur, I am sure, that this situation could very easily lead to the downfall of the National Youth Service and the collapse of your socialist ideals. Either that, or you will find that you yourself will be required to put your money where your mouth is."

"Money?"

"It is an idiomatic phrase, Monsieur Albert. It means that you will have to do your share of toilet cleaning too, in order to maintain credibility."

It was clear that I had impressed not only myself, but also my dumbstruck audience.

"In short, Monsieur, with the greatest of respect, we are not cleaning the toilets. We are teachers. We and indeed, you, will be in breach of contract. And we will be forced take action." Carol could not resist having the final word.

Monsieur Albert sniffed. He picked up the telephone and spoke to his secretary, who slouched in and opened a book on his desk, pointing out a number. He dialled it and spoke in Creole, adjusting his pronunciation and syntax so that we had no clue about what he was saying, especially when it mattered. When he put the phone down, a small smile lit the lower half of his face, while his eyes remained cold. "The situation has been resolved. I will inform all staff of my decision within the hour."

Carol stood up, turned and left, saying a barely audible thank you and goodbye, while I leaned forward and shook Monsieur Albert's hand, announcing that I was glad we had managed to sort things out so easily.

"What the hell was the Arthur Scargill speech all about?" asked Carol, when we were outside.

"Oh, you know," I simpered, "just giving him the benefit of my informed opinion."

"Well, I hope he didn't recognise the dullard beneath the swagger. I'd like to stay on a bit longer!"

As usual, Carol doubted my approach. I said I would go back and explain that I had only been trying to help, but Carol said she would throttle me if I did.

Rose was up to speed before I got back to the staff room. She couldn't keep still. All eyes were on me, and I bowed a little, sensing the crowd's quiet approbation.

"What did you do?" she asked. "We don't have to clean the toilets if we don't want to! The cleaner is coming back next week!"

The secretary had moved fast and was now slinking back to her office adjoining the headmaster's.

It turned out that said cleaner had been taken sick with a chill, after stepping out into the rain for a moment. Monsieur Albert had encouraged her to cut short the usual two-week period of convalescence and return to perform her essential and valued duties.

"Well done!" said Rose, squeezing my hand.

Later that day, there was a request for voluntary help to keep the staff conveniences hygienic until her return. I didn't sign the list, but practically everyone else did. It was at that point that it began to dawn on me that my negotiating skills might have been rather heavy handed. If everyone else was prepared to lend a hand, then why not me?

"Happy now?" Carol said, over a particularly essential cup of tea after work.

"Do you think we'll get the sack?" I was miserable and needed comforting.

"*We?*" replied my best and bosom buddy, who would stick with me through hell and high water. "You're the gormless dimwit, not *me!*"

It wasn't the response I had been hoping for.

Death by Coconut

The u-bend embarrassment seemed to have been flushed away (sorry, sometimes I can't help myself), and the headmaster still greeted me with the same clipped professionalism as before. My behaviour had been tolerated and I would not transgress the rules of a socialist ethos a second time. Well, not on purpose, anyway.

It was coming up to payday and we were planning a barbeque on the beach, hosted by the teachers who lived in the beach houses at Beau Vallon. The planning committee was headed by Penny and Dick and mainly involved the application of some good old Yorkshire skin-flintery.

"We will provide the venue. You folk can bring the fish and meat. Oh, and don't forget the wine. And we'll need bread. Salad would be good, too."

Carol said she thought she might have to drown Penny at some point and asked me to ensure that, in the event that anyone deemed her actions unwarranted enough to put her behind bars, I inform Dave so that he could come and sort it out.

"I'll never let them take you!" I cried.

"Just leave it to Dave, thanks. I don't want to end up with a life sentence, in solitary confinement."

I laughed heartily at yet another of Carol's priceless jokes.

The barbeque was postponed at the last minute, due to sickness and diarrhoea striking down a significant number of our group. Also, Rose's beach house had been broken into and she was livid. I would ask her about it the following week.

For now, as Carol and I had escaped the chore of shopping for a party we didn't really want to attend, we were left wondering what to do with our weekend.

"We should go out on our own," suggested Carol.

"Yeah! I'd love that!" I had a surge of happiness. We had spent a lot of our leisure time in the company of our new friends and it would make a change just to chill out with Carol.

"Fancy going to the beach? We could take a picnic, something tasty but light, not too sticky, and some beers, cold, don't forget the bottle opener, or the *chatini* (*chatini* was our new thing – green papaya sliced thinly and pickled, we had it with everything). Oh, and remember the napkins, sweetie."

"Oh, Lordy! Whatever shall we do? We seem to have run out!"

"Just stick a loo roll in, then," Carol suggested.

"How coarse you are, my lovely Devonshire trollop."

It would be bliss. Just the two of us! Carol opened up the fridge, in search of picnic fodder.

"I'll get the rucksack and the swimming stuff,"
I said, wondering whether I should shave my legs.

"Put some sun cream in."

"Okey dokey, Mrs. Pokey."

"Put a tape on, too."

Dancing to *The Who*, we whirled a selection of
edibles into pots and wrappers, helping Roger
Daltrey from time to time with heartfelt emotional
outbursts. Could Tommy hear him? Tommy!
Can you hear me? To-o-o-my…

"Do you think Elton minded?" I asked.

"What? Being the deaf, dumb and blind kid?"

"Yeah."

Carol swung around and struck a pose. "Nah.
You've just got to remember that …he sure plays
a mean pinbaaaaaaall!" She couldn't sing. But
that didn't stop her.

My devoted pal was great at sneaking off, as I
may have already mentioned.

"Just need a couple of sarnies. You do those
and I'll whip round the old bod with a razor." She
disappeared, leaving me to finish the eclectic cold
collation and to clean up the mess she'd made.

I collected the rubbish and approached the bin
at the other end of the kitchen. That's when I
noticed the mild aroma of something beginning to
decompose, just after I'd caught sight of about a
billion ants on a mission.

"Carol!"

"Shitting hell! Can't I have a minute!" she
said, arriving with one leg lathered up.

"Look!"

It was one of our lizards. It had crawled inside an empty juice bottle and languished there, inside the bin, unable to climb back. Its body was shrivelled, its eyes fixed, its tiny feet shrunken. The ants marched up the bottle, down inside and back out, presumably carrying off their putrefied lizard lunch, exiting under the kitchen door, down the steps, neat and determined, until they disappeared under the foundations of the house.

Carol tutted and took over. I kept to the other end of the room, trying to avoid thinking about the disgusting notion of Uncle Ernie fiddling about with Elton, and putting together a couple of salami baps. We hoped we would remember never to leave bottles in the upright position again.

We got a lift down to the beach with a rare passing car. It was too hot to walk, carrying our, as yet unused, compact and bijou cool box. Our driver wanted to know whether we would enjoy some company, but we could see that he knew from the start that he would be out of luck. We got out on the coastal road just as he had run out of innuendo and was about to take more direct action.

"This'll do. Thanks mate," said Carol.

Here we were. *The Fifth of June Road.*

"When did the Seychelles become independent?" Unfortunately, I seemed to have voiced my musings, leaving me wide open to inevitable ridicule.

Carol looked at me, "1976, some time in June. The road's named after the coup d'état, you birdbrain!"

"Is that when René took over?" I knew it was, but I wanted to humour her.

"Yeah. I was talking to Anka about it. She was here when it happened. Said it came over the radio, couple of people were killed, and then there were curfews for a while. Tanzania got involved and sent over their military to support René. Armed soldiers on the streets. Very unnerving. She said that Mancham was accused of caring more about foreigners than the people of the Seychelles. René would change all that, he promised – sent some Brits home under military escort to the airport, apparently."

"Blimey!" I thought about the comments I'd made to Monsieur Albert with a new understanding that made me regret my rebellious tone.

"Anyway, despite the promise of a new socialist régime, René declared a one-party state, not long before the elections – of course he won. No one in opposition. Anyway, he was seen by many as a bit of a sneak, not to mention a dictator. Not surprising, really. Stacking the cards like that. Seems to have calmed down a bit nowadays, but I reckon there's still a lot of bad feeling left over. So, next time we have a run-in with the authorities, keep your flippin' trap shut!"

"Why didn't you tell me all this before?" I whimpered.

"Thought you already knew! Now stop sulking. It'll be fine, don't worry about it! If they deport you, I'll help carry your bags to the plane."

I couldn't be depressed for long, not with the beach spread out before us and the ocean as a backdrop. It was so picture perfect that Carol felt duty bound to pinch me to make sure we weren't dreaming.

Our beach was the type that you see in holiday brochures for destinations so chic and fabulous that you don't even bother looking at the prices. If you're not minted, or over sixty and going on that holiday you've always promised yourself, the Seychelles would remain confined to that most essential area of the human brain where wild cravings are kept. Mine were Sting-based scenarios, while Carol preferred a bit of Adam Antery.

Ahead of us, as far as the next bay, the beach was practically ours. Pristine, devoid of sun loungers, bars, dogs, children or lobster-coloured Brits.

I could tell you once more about the porcelain-coloured sand with its texture of soft sugar, or the gentle ocean breeze that disturbed our hair just the right amount, or the blue, blue water, finished with a delicate lace froth reminiscent of delicious cocktails I had sipped at The Coconut Grove in London's West End. You might get a little bit fed up if I went on any more about the rustle of the palm fronds and the gentle thud of coconuts falling…

"Bugger me! That was a bit close for comfort!" Carol had stopped to inspect a coconut that had fallen a good five or six metres in front of her.

I couldn't help inventing a statistic: "Did you know that over one hundred people a year are killed by falling coconuts?"

Carol didn't even bother to look round at me. "That would be where?"

Easy question. Easy answer. "Here, in the Seychelles."

"Really? And how many people live in the Seychelles?"

This was trickier, but I was committed. I thought of the population of Cambridge and added a bit on. "I believe it's about one hundred thousand, all told."

"Sixty-five thousand, actually. So that means that the odds of anyone dying from a blow to the head by being struck by a rogue coconut, are around 1:650, including babies, toddlers, the old and infirm, not to mention those who are allergic to sun, sand or coconuts, which compares to the odds of dying from drowning in the bath, coming out at around 1:600." Carol picked up the coconut and shook it.

"I didn't know you could drown in the bath. Gosh. Is that really true?"

"Of course it isn't. I just made it up, like you did."

I can attest to the fact that a coconut in the small of the back can fell a large mammal trying to escape impact by running across a sandy beach. And it hurts. A lot.

We walked north, finding some shade and risking death by coconut on several occasions. We talked about everything under the sun: men, travel, jobs, biscuits and took care to avoid the subject of politics. We reminisced about our times in France and our croupier jobs with London Playboy, embroidering the past whilst luxuriating in the present. We agreed that we had had the most fun together and that we were lucky. So lucky... Then we got hungry.

"Let's eat!" said Carol.

I persuaded her to come for a swim first. The water would be warm, but when we came out, the breeze would cool us. Fish swam close to us, and we could see for metres in every direction. The water was not deep, but it was okay for swimming.

"Dragan said there are lots of sharks in these waters," said Carol, looking out to sea over my left shoulder.

"I know. But they're not the type that attack. Even *I* know that."

It turned out that, although I was right, on the whole, Dragan had witnessed the aftermath of an attack in which a tourist had died. The victim had been swimming at Anse Boileau with her husband and young daughter when a shark, which was apparently not plankton eating, bit her in half at the waist. Dragan had been alerted by the screams and had gone down to help.

It was a sobering image, even if it were

-

-

probably untrue, and I wished Carol hadn't planted it forever in my sensitive brain. Suddenly, I didn't feel quite so comfortable in the water, and started to make for the shore, slowly at first, until panic took over and made me move as fast as I could, unconcerned about other hazards like stone fish or a stubbed toe. Carol chased me, making what she called 'shark noises'.

We settled, still giggling with relief, under our selected tree, and gasped for a while, catching our breath.

"Tell me again, what have we got?" asked Carol.

"Cold fish, salami sandwiches with chilli sauce, tomato salad, cheese triangles, *gateau piment* and *chatini*," I said, enthusiastically. "And there's fresh paw paw with lime for afters."

It sounded nasty, but it tasted delicious. All of it. The white fish had been bought from the market in quantities big enough to feed the proverbial army. I had frozen some of it and baked the rest with ginger and garlic. It tasted like no fish I'd ever eaten in England. The texture was meaty and at the same time creamy.

"Well I never!" said Carol, rubbing her soft, round belly.

"Nice. Perfect."

The sun would set at around six, so we spread out to soak up a few rays and do some gentle reading. Just as we had done on the beaches of southern France almost ten years earlier. It wasn't long before I dozed off, only to be woken by Carol's swearing.

"Fucking little bastards!"

I wondered who could have irritated her so much, after all, we hadn't seen more than a handful of people on the bit of the beach we had covered.

"Quick! Get them off your legs! Christ, they itch like buggery!"

I looked down at my legs. At first I didn't notice much. Then, I saw lots of little red blobs appearing as I watched. I tried to brush some of them off and squashed them. I was soon hopping around with Carol, slapping and cursing. We had been attacked by sand flies and Carol was right about the itching. Into the sea we went, which helped a little. But by the time we staggered back to the road and had hitched our way back, I had very little skin left below the knee and a great deal more than usual under my fingernails.

They came out just before sunset or in the shade, on or near the beach, apparently. I decided that, henceforth, we would not. When we got home, we doused our bites in Icebreaker for want of TCP and drank the rest. It did the trick.

Motorbike Heaven

"Fish and rice, very nice. Rice and fish, what a dish!" The chant went up in the classrooms just before lunch and died down as the students approached the canteen, under the eagle eyes of the inappropriately named *animateurs*. The students were brave, but not that brave.

There was generally a set menu, although we did occasionally get chicken. I became used to eating any part of fish or fowl, preferring to ingest without too much thought. I had a vague feeling of guilt, which arose from the notion that, despite the fact that Seychelles was proudly independent, it was still poor. The food was basic and the portions frugal, which thought led on to more difficult moral dilemmas in the society I felt so little a part of. So, I didn't complain. I dislodged surprisingly tasty flesh from fish heads and sucked on chicken bones, trying to work out which of the servers hated me most, from the size of the body parts that appeared on my plate. Did I mention that the students acted as waitresses, too? Some of the teachers got more than they could eat. Rose and I were not among them.

"I heard that a Swedish boy is selling his motorbike," said Rose, at one such lunch, as our plates were taken away to be washed and put away by the *responsab* washers-up of the day.

"I don't think we want a motorbike," I replied, thinking as I said it, that it might actually be a very good idea. "Is it any good, do you know?"

"I can get you his address and telephone number if you like, and you can go and see it." Rose always looked delighted about everything, especially if she'd helped anyone out.

"Great stuff! Thanks Rose. Might be fun!"

The Swedish boy was about thirty-five, and was from Norway. He had a Kawasaki 250cc motorbike for sale that looked as though it might have been left over from a very bad war film. 'As new' it wasn't, in fact, I doubted whether there was a category in any motorbike magazine that could be applied to Benedikt's less than alluring offering.

Carol and I arrived to find him working on said bike, which made us very nervous. If it were broken now, what would happen when we got it home? He did have a 'genuine reason for sale' – it was standing just a little further up the hill, looking extremely Italian, leaning to one side on its stand, blood red and shiny as a blister. It looked as though Benedikt was clearing out the garage to make way for his new purchase.

"Have you ridden before?" he enquired, politely. I could tell from the enigmatic lines on his forehead and the way he held my gaze for less than a second that he thought me less than competent.

"Yes. I had a Lambretta some years ago."

"What size?"

I knew enough not to answer 'large' or 'two-seater' and I thought it had been a 50cc. However, I wasn't sure that I should mention this last fact, as it was probably a laughable prospect to anyone serious about motorbikes.

"250," I said.

"Wow! That's great. You should be fine, then."

I had obviously given the wrong answer, and I heard my grandmother telling me that pride comes before a fall, not to spoil a nice day, and you *can* if you *may,* Miss Spicer… I told my brain to *stop*!

"Do you ride?" Benedikt was speaking to Carol, who had gone over to look at the newer, more impressive machine.

"Nope. Don't drive either." That was the end of *that* conversation.

The sun was hot and I had a quick confab with Carol to see what she wanted to do. We decided that we would take it out for a spin.

Benedikt gave me a helmet, saying that I should go alone to start with, to get the feel of it. This sounded like good advice. As it happened, the old adage about bicycles and never forgetting how to ride one, held true for motorbikes too, except when it came to changing gear and balancing at the same time. The most terrifying part was the steep rise from the road to his house, which looked like some kind of death slide as I started up the bike and edged down, wobbling and saying a silent prayer, my eyes on the road below, hoping that no vehicles would pass by at a crucial moment and flatten me. Goodness knows what quiet thoughts of catastrophe were going through Benedikt's mind as he observed a scatty

Englishwoman he had only just met, meandering at an acute angle towards almost certain death.

Against all odds, I arrived at The Fifth of June Road intact, if suffering with what I took to be the early signs of an imminent heart attack. My arms felt tingly, my legs were at around fifty per cent responsiveness, and I had what I assumed to be palpitations. Nevertheless, I indicated right and turned out on the, thankfully, deserted tarmac. It wasn't long before I remembered what to do, and I passed into the infinitely more dangerous phase characterised by an enormous amount of misplaced confidence brought on by the thrill of the open road. It was amazing. Speed was my drug of choice. "*Poop poop*," I murmured, "*poop, poop!*"

When I got back, zooming up the incline and imagining the wheelie I would like to perform, Carol and Benedikt gave me a round of applause and I grinned.

"How much do you want for it?" I asked.

"£300," said Benedikt. "I don't want rupees."

It was an outrageous price, but not by Seychelles standards. Penny's Mini Moke had cost almost £2,000. I hoped that her assertion that she would get more for it when they left held true for ancient motorbikes.

"Throw in the helmet?"

"Sure. Think I have another inside, if you want it."

"Done!"

Carol took my fairly presentable helmet and I had the other much more manky one, which would not fit her, she alleged. The bike was slightly less manoeuvrable with a pillion but, with time, would be almost as enjoyable.

"Hold on tight," I said.

"I am, you fool!" shouted Carol, over the roar of the engine.

I drove home, as pleased as a child with a new toy, not caring about the cheque I had signed for my last bit of savings. It was good to be alive. It was great to have our own transport. It was interesting to have a crawling sensation inside my helmet. Just a minute. Strike that last comment. There was definitely something moving against my scalp, and then a trail of creepy-crawlies emerged onto my forehead. I thought 'spider!' I thought 'centipede!' I screamed and stopped the bike, ripped off the helmet and saw, to my relative delight, hundreds of ants, which had, until that moment been living quietly in the lining.

"Glad I didn't have that one," said Carol.

Benedikt had told me he often rode without a helmet. The police didn't care about that kind of thing, he said. So, when the ants had stopped swarming a little, Carol agreed to hold on to it and I let the wind blow through my golden locks. Carol didn't like that, either.

At home, after I had opened up the enormous garage and placed our new acquisition slap bang in the middle of it, I took the helmet out onto the balcony and sprayed it with *Doom*, a product that I suspected was banned in almost every country in the world. It did the trick.

"Icebreaker?" suggested Carol.

"With coke?"

"Yeah."

"Why the hell not! Make it a treble and go easy on the coke."

Volcanoes, Frank Sinatra and P.A.Y.E

Teaching was going well. The girls and I had found our routine and, as long as I allowed a few of them to doze off unobtrusively, the rest of them were willing to toe the line, especially if it involved singing or larking about a bit. The only problem with this was that the class next door would be writing an essay on whatever the teacher had written up on the board at the beginning of the lesson. That's all they seemed to do, it seemed to me. I rarely heard the teacher speak. The sound of my class having a bit of fun would probably not affect the students too much, but might very well cause the teacher to lose count of her stitches.

Rose said that the knitting circle had deemed modern methods of education to be unworthy, assuring me that it was because they were deeply afraid of anything new, and frightened that they may be called upon to change their own, brain-shrivelling approach. The fact that I was an arrogant bugger, with little respect for other people's ideas on education, was something I had still not fully grasped.

I didn't want to interfere with them and I concluded that, as long as the status quo continued, they probably didn't want to interfere with me. It would be a standoff. No further action would be taken. They were wrong and I

-
109
-

was right. No point in rubbing it in.

It was around this time that I noticed one of my students had been missing for rather longer than was usual, so I put in a report to the school administration. I was informed in due course that Laureen had gone back to her island home and would not be returning.

"She's pregnant," Rose told me.

"*What*?" I said. "She's fifteen!"

"It happens here," replied Rose. "And I think fifteen is old enough."

It was a sobering thought. I knew that there were countries where the age of consent was considerably lower. I pictured Laureen at her desk, chewing the end of her pencil while she thought about the exercise she was doing.

"What will happen to her?"

"It depends on the family. She will probably have an abortion."

I remembered Miriam.

"Will she never come back to school?"

"Generally, the girls who are sent away stay on their island. Don't worry. She will be fine."

It didn't seem fair. That would be it, for Laureen. No education, no choice. If she wanted to stay on the island, that was up to her, but if she wanted a career of some kind... I longed to say something, to protest on Laureen's behalf, but Rose persuaded me not to, assuring me that it would make no difference. Bearing in mind the fact that I had already labelled myself as a troublemaker, I am ashamed to say that, after the story had run its course, after the various expressions of sympathy had been weighed and counted, I did nothing. Laureen was not the first to suffer such flagrant discrimination, and she would not be the last.

The weekend arrived and the re-scheduled barbeque loomed. We would have to go shopping in Victoria. The bike was running well and I had become a moderately competent rider. We had discovered that two girls riding a motorbike in the Seychelles attracted the attention of other drivers, who often shouted compliments to us as they forced us off the road. Luckily, we didn't understand most of them.

The other 'followers' were a lot more unnerving. Carol had taken the advice of a friend and now carried a large stick, like some kind of medieval jouster, in order to defend our ankles from the stray dogs, who ran out in an explosion of barking and bloodlust. The first time this happened I very nearly lost control. Now, we were ready to do battle. I felt sorry for the half-starved creatures, but there were no such things as animal shelters in the Seychelles.

We set off for the shops before lunch. It had rained in the night, leaving a layer of additional moisture in the air, rising up from the forest. I never really liked the heavy odour of exotic plant life, but I do remember the smells and can taste the verdant saturation in the back of my throat even now. I occasionally longed for a proper autumn, with the more familiar smell of damp leaves rising from the muddy shadows in a good old country park in England. A life without seasons could only be temporary.

Carol put on the large, empty rucksack (which now gave off a fishy aroma) that we would use to carry back the shopping and I checked we had sufficient cash. We had almost run out and, as it had been rumoured that we had been paid the week before, we would visit the bank in town and withdraw some cash. The bike drummed along the winding road as I avoided potholes and thought about what we would need to buy, all the time not quite believing that I was riding a motorbike on an island in the middle of the Indian Ocean, with Carol behind me no doubt thinking exactly the same thing. Life was surreal. I imagined the volcano beneath us that had produced the granite islands. I looked up the steep wooded slopes and wondered whether it would blow before we got to the shops, imagining how it would feel to be blasted into the atmosphere and incinerated, or perhaps thrown to safety on a flimsy outcrop of rocks, waiting for the secondary eruption. We would wait to die, Carol and I, like Frank Sinatra and his buddy in *The Devil at Four O'clock*. It would be tragic. It would be epic.

"Hurry up! I need a wee!" shouted Carol.

Lovely Carol, my bosom buddy. I imagined her with half a bridge crushing her chest, listening to my wise words of consolation. We hit a bump.

"Shit. Too late!"

When Carol had dried off, we went to the market, wandering around the tables set out with

mounds of colourful wares it was hard to imagine
a use for. The place was busy and noisy.
Chaotic. We bought vegetables and fruit, some of
which we recognised and others to try. There was
fish, but Carol said she didn't want to carry a
whole one in the bag, so we opted for some meat
from the supermarket. Frozen was cheaper than
fresh, and we ended up with a rather suspect slab
of beef, well wrapped and hopefully edible.

"What about salad? And they said we should
bring bread."

"Rose said the Frenchies would bring bread."

"Makes sense."

We were done. There was time for a visit to
the *Pirate's Arms* in the centre of town for a
coffee and, in the end, we decided to stay for
lunch – aubergine fritters and pickles. It was
perhaps the only large meeting place in Victoria
and resembled a huge open pub/canteen, basic but
welcoming. We recognised some people, but kept
ourselves to ourselves, looking out on the street at
the generally ancient and surprisingly still
functioning vehicles passing by. Very few new
vehicles, if any, were to be seen. Imports from
the African mainland were treasured and nurtured,
repaired and made good. Never scrapped. A
woman in a colourful sari passed by, followed by
an elegant, tall woman with African headdress,
then a man with ebony skin, wearing a blue tee
shirt and beige shorts, each one encapsulating a
culture, all citizens of the islands. I seldom saw
any tourists. In those days, most people tended to
stay at their five-star resorts most of the time or

go out into the jungle on guided tours of the island. The streets, with their clatter and sprawl, belonged to the Seychellois.

It made a change not to be eating fish and rice. The fritters were good. I would have liked to order more, but Carol wanted to check we were solvent. It was time to get to the bank, where our accounts would have been credited with a salary commensurate with our experience and expertise – mediocre. The pay had not been the deciding factor in our decision to come to paradise, but it would be plenty for us to cover our expenses and put some aside for travelling.

"This is it," said Carol.

It looked like a bank. And it was.

Inside, we withdrew what we needed and asked for a balance.

"There must be some mistake," I said to the clerk, who was already yawning.

"No, madam. The statement is correct."

"This figure is much too low," I insisted.

"It is your salary, madam. Paid by the National Youth Service, in pounds."

I was not looking for a definition, I was looking for the missing £600 or so that would make the total recognisable.

"Shit!" said Carol, finally noticing the shortfall.

The assistant looked suitably shocked.

"Could we speak to the manager, please?"

It was all terribly simple, the manager explained. The salary that we had been offered was gross and the salary we received was net.

Surely that was how it worked in most of the countries in the world? It was of course no surprise to us that deductions had been applied to our earnings; it was the amount of these deductions that was the problem. The difference between the gross and the net was forty per cent - we were high earners and living in a poor country. What did we expect? I considered the look in the bank manager's eye and tried to interpret it, in vain. Perhaps it was sympathy, perhaps it was national pride, perhaps it was scorn. Whatever it was, there was no point in arguing with it.

The shrinking of our disposable income was the first surprise. The next one would be even more sobering.

A Beach Party and some Bad News

The barbeque was lit and the sun was setting. Penny and Dick were in charge of the booze, which mainly consisted of Icebreaker and fruit juice. There was even ice. It seemed that our hosts were not as mean-spirited as we had imagined.

All the usual people were there, plus a few others we hadn't met. I searched the crowd for Sven and saw him standing in the surf, holding Marianne's hand, with a bottle of Seybrew in the other. Marc came over to compliment us and to get away from Penny, who obviously fancied him.

"My God! She is a married woman! Can't she behave herself?" Neither of us had the answer to that one.

"I thought you came from a country where passion knows no bounds!" I said. Carol rolled her eyes. Marc didn't quite understand.

"She means that Frenchmen are famous for their infidelity, and for not possessing a toothbrush," explained Carol.

Marc took exception to both of these statements. Carol would not apologise and so I left them to it and went to get another drink.

"How's it going, Dick?"

He looked startled. Penny was not around to answer for him. He blew through his teeth and laughed. "Oh, you know! It's always the man's job to do the barbeque!"

"Great stuff! Keep it up!" I wished, with all

my heart that I hadn't said that. Luckily, Dick was not used to innuendo coming from anyone other than his wife, or else he knew that I had made a fatal error and had decided to spare my embarrassment.

"Right!" He laughed through his nose, this time, fast and sniffy.

I went over to the house and poured myself a large rum. Anka was inside, getting more ice. Dragan, had gone for a walk. There were questions I was dying to ask, but I didn't dare.

"Are you serious about Sven?" she said, her long fingers pressing out the cubes into a bowl.

"What?" So much for propriety!

She gave me a look.

"I…"

"It doesn't matter. If you don't want to talk about it."

"I…"

She sliced up a mango and squeezed it into our drinks through her fingers."

"I like him," I admitted, finally.

We sat down at the kitchen table.

"He's no good. But he is beautiful." Anka took out a cigarette and put her head back, stroking her neck, before inserting it into her mouth and lighting up, the flame catching something I hadn't seen before in her eyes. A sort of vulnerability.

"What about Carol?"

"She doesn't fancy him."

Anka shook her head and I realised that I had misinterpreted her question.

"Oh. She has an off/on relationship with a farmer in the North of England." This made us both laugh.

"Marianne doesn't know, you know? She is very trusting," Anka said, after a moment. "He is discreet." Her eyes were alive with emotion. And it came to me that she and Sven might have a history too.

"Oh," I replied. It occurred to me that Anka was the only person I'd met who had shown any concern for Marianne's feelings.

"Let's hope the bastard gets stung back one day! And, don't worry, it you want him – go for it. I don't care! I say good luck to you. Marianne should get rid of the little toad! Fuck! Let's eat."

Some of the barbeque food was ready and Dick was giving out burgers and slices of our steak, under strict supervision. There was bread, provided by Rose, along with a breadfruit dish made with cheese and cream, which was delicious. The French contingent had brought nothing, but Marc had taken out a boat and come back with an enormous fish, which he duly gutted and slammed on the fire, much to Dick's consternation.

Emile and Thierry had settled on the sand with Rose and Carol, so I went over with my food and joined them.

"Emile says we're invited to stay in the French house on Praslin, one weekend before Christmas," said Carol, delightedly, the glow from a small lamp lighting her strong, angular cheekbones.

"Yeah! It will be fun!" said Thierry.

"There are five bedrooms and it has a kitchen – we can cook and have a party," added Emile.

"Sounds good. Where is Praslin? And how do we get there?" asked Carol.

"You are so practical!" Marc laughed and kissed her on the cheek. So un-French!

It was true. Information like that could wait. It was enough that there were islands out there for us to visit, stepping stones to a trip to Mauritius, Madagascar, Africa. Adventure – so much of it, I felt as though I would burst with joy. In the soft light of the moon and the scattered manmade flicker of oil lamps, we looked like beings from another world, communicating in ways so varied and subtle that an observer could easily have philosophised over the significance of the patterns we formed, our gesticulations and expressions. I savoured such moments, when the ordinary world seemed unimportant and remote. This was life. It was the closest feeling to peace, almost to enlightenment, that I had ever experienced.

The chat shifted inevitably to work, contracts and the future. Our voices became stronger. We were derogatory, outraged and smug by turns. Derogatory about the French salaries and benefits, which were enormous, outraged about the time we had to get up in the mornings and the time we got home at night, and smug to be sitting on a beautiful beach, listening to the waves, sipping rum and eating fish that had literally been plucked from the clearest waters on Earth.

After we'd eaten, wiping our plates with bread and licking our fingers, we noticed that there was something going on in front of Penny and Dick's house. Lots of lanterns had been placed on the veranda and, with the moon and the myriad stars, visibility was good enough. A ball was fetched and teams were chosen. Goals were marked out with odd clothing, and lines were drawn in the sand. Dick whistled impressively and the game began. We moved closer and refilled our glasses, cheering and hooting as small knots of players formed around the ball. There were some girls playing, including Penny, who had put on a pair of shorts and a very skimpy tee shirt. Before long, it became obvious that she was keen to tackle Marc whenever possible. We nudged each other and enjoyed the increasing hilarity, as she flirted and squealed her way around the pitch. Players fell, players dived. Dick did his bit to referee the game, all the time forced to observe the wild advances Penny was making towards Marc.

"Do you think he'll murder her in her bed?" I asked Carol.

"Somebody ought to," she slurred and promptly threw her arms in the air. "Goal!"

Marc looked over and grinned. Carol jumped up, danced around and fell over.

"Rose says we are not allowed to travel far," said Carol, drunk as a skunk and about to try to put on her helmet back to front, for the drive home. The party was over.

"What do you mean, you lovely dullard?"

She belched and put her spiralling eyes in

front of mine, a finger to her lips and explained, fairly laboriously, with frequent pauses, that our contracts forbade us to go to Africa.

"What are you talking about?" I cried, laughing, but at the same time sensing that there might be a grain of truth in her rantings.

"Shhh! You'll wake up the turtles. Come here." Carol wanted a cuddle. "There, there. We are prisoners. You and me. Hee hee! Never mind. It's … all right. We can have a nice cup of tea when we get home. Where's Marc? Marc! Where are you?"

If I didn't get her on the bike soon, she would fall into a drunken coma, right there on the beach.

"Do you need help?" Marc approached, his keys jangling.

"Please. Carol's off her rocker. Talking rubbish."

"Marc. You scored a goal! Let me give you a big kiss!"

Marc held her up and laughed when she missed his mouth completely.

"She says we can't go to Africa!" I said, shaking my head.

"Ah, no. Yes, she is right. We can go to Mauritius and the other Seychelles islands. Not Africa. No."

"Madagascar?"

"No."

The bellow I let out was loud enough to bring Penny and Dick running. They confirmed it. It was written into our contracts. The reasons were political. They would tell me another time.

-
-

It was too much. First the pay cut and now this! It was too much. Much too much. I rode home sober in body and in mind, unable to appreciate the beauty of the night.

Time for Action

And so it came to be that Carol and I and the NYS were no longer best friends.

We made an appointment to see John, the person who had interviewed us in London and who had an office on Mahé at the NYS headquarters. The person who had tricked us!

He was not expecting our complaints and was genuinely baffled and concerned that we believed he may have misinformed us in some way. Misinformed! I served up a very large piece of my mind to the poor man and Carol made it seem like a meagre snack. We were disappointed, we were distraught, we had come to the Seychelles with the intention of exploring and we had been taken for a ride, led up the garden path, duped and swindled! Not only could we not afford to put on the air conditioning, but neither could we hope to save up the airfares for the trips we had been planning to take and now could not! I was adamant, if confused. We were stranded.

"Stranded in the Seychelles! Sounds like a good title for a book," said Carol, with a laugh that was tragic.

John apologised and hoped that we would come around; after all, we had come to assist in the emancipation of the Seychelles. It was a third world country, exploited throughout its history and currently rich pickings for wealthy developers from South Africa. Together, we would be part of an exciting future, endeavouring to ensure that the islands evolved into a fair and ethically sound independent nation. It was a seductive vision and, as we were not heartless, we did see the bright side of our predicament. However, more pressing was the fact that our freedom was being restricted. Our democratic right to free movement had been curtailed. We dug our heels in and said, finally, that we wanted to hand in our notice with immediate effect. Luckily for us, nothing immediate ever happened in the Indian Ocean. It would take in excess of three months to get the ball rolling. In the meantime, we would negotiate a more productive use of our remaining time in paradise and, ironically, enjoy our stay all the more for its temporary nature.

On Ste. Anne there was a different buzz in the staff room. Goodness knows what juicy tidbit the knitting circle was presiding over. Rose said they sounded like a murder of crows, invigorated by a tasty cadaver. I was impressed by her knowledge of collective nouns and her use of advanced vocabulary.

"They know you are leaving, but they don't know when or why. It's driving them mad!" she laughed, at coffee break.

"Are you going to tell them?" I asked.

"No! It's too much fun to listen to their theories. Do you know that Serena thinks you are pregnant?" Rose's eyes expanded, her irises once again floating in a milky sea.

"Ha!" And then I wondered if they had an idea

who the father might be.

"You won't believe it."

"Marc?"

"No! They don't know Marc!" She was giggling.

"David?"

Rose gasped and put her hand to her mouth. David was the very old and very kind resident handy man.

"Who, then?"

"The headmaster!" she spluttered.

It was my turn to be surprised. And a little flattered, to be honest. They obviously considered me top notch totty.

"It's only because you are white!" said Rose. Own goal! I thought. "Yeah. Of course." I nodded.

Carol thought it was hilarious, predictably. On the other campus, there had been gossip too, that our methods were unorthodox and we were being dismissed for our lack of discipline in the classroom. This was probably a fair assessment, although we did have our successes, too.

The students knew something. It was subtly evident from their more sober attention to the lesson and their overly enthusiastic participation in group work. I said nothing to them, on the basis that I myself had no idea what was going to happen to me. Carol and I had drafted a letter of resignation in which we requested a termination of our one-year contract, due to misinformation at interview. We assumed that we would be released in due course and issued with a return ticket to England. We had got over our initial disgust, and bore no ill feelings towards anyone. It was simply that we did not want to spend a whole year unable to move freely.

In the meantime, Rose invited me for a meal at her bungalow in Beau Vallon. Carol said she didn't care what I did, or whom I did it with. So I set out on the bike alone the following Saturday afternoon, leaving my bosom buddy on the balcony, sulking.

"Why don't you come too?" I had suggested.

"Bog off and enjoy yourself!"

I knew from experience that I could not win, and so I bogged off, as advised, slightly nervous to be travelling alone, but at the same time, with a fullness in my chest that was either excitement or (more likely) indigestion. The spirit of adventure was strong in me, I'll admit, and the views along the coast seemed different without someone looking over my shoulder. There were outcrops of rocks, some gigantic – how had they got there? It was hard to imagine the violence that must have formed the tranquil scenes that now passed before me. The odd fisherman stood on the beach or sat in a boat, their lines dangling for dinner, occasionally children appeared, in the middle of the road, or playing on the beach. The human element brought comfort and added poignancy.

It was another beautiful day, with the usual white clouds massing into cumulonimbus in a sea of overhead blue that made me breathe deeply and grin at the joy of a simple life.

I considered the people I saw, only now pondering the effects of a new prosperity coming to the islands and their inhabitants. It was a country that had been occupied by the French and the British, where slavery had thrived. Now, the changes were coming thick and fast. I remembered my students, fresh from remote islands, where life must be basic, aspirations few, suddenly transported away from their homes, dressed in the uniform of the NYS and expected to find jobs to earn money and improve their prospects.

The government, which had been formed illegally in 1977, was now itself vulnerable, and there had already been a failed military coup while we were there. We had seen soldiers and police on the road into Victoria, checking cars after the act, looking for who knows what. They had guns and nervous expressions on their faces. Nervous, yet bemused. It had been strange to be 'in' the news, to have been present at an event that would be reported all over the world. In some ways, being so close meant that information was not as readily available. René was still in power, nothing had changed. Yet.

I drummed and joggled along, my mind running free, hoping that Carol would not miss me too much, wondering whether I would ever see Sven again and, inexplicably, thinking about my father, flying gliders on a mountain on the Welsh border called the Long Mynd.

A Visit to Rose's House

It was a truly lovely setting. Beau Vallon was aptly named. A large sweep of white sand, bordered by lush palm trees and, dominating the view, the shallow waters of the Indian Ocean, shelving into unimaginable depths, alive with extraordinary creatures.

Rose's bungalow was the nearest one to the sea, in a set of about five or six, as far as I can remember. Penny and Dick lived in another group, a bit further along the beach.

The door was open.

"Hi, Rose?"

She appeared, wearing a frilly apron and a huge smile, her dark skin shining with health, happiness and moisturiser.

"Oh! You are here!" she said, delightedly. It suddenly occurred to me that she had thought I might not come.

"Something smells good," I said, hugging her.

"It's just curry," she said, grinning.

"Do you want any help?"

"No. We should have a drink. Or would you like to swim?"

We changed into our costumes and I went out deep enough to swim, while Rose stayed in the shallows and watched. She had never learned to swim and didn't want me to teach her. The water was not very clear, as the sand had been churned up by the currents. Until December, we would have storms and angry skies from time to time, but the temperature would remain at around twenty-nine degrees in the daytime and there would be copious amounts of sunshine.

Rose ran back to the house and brought me a towel. We sat on the sand while she told me about her family in Mauritius and why she had come to the Seychelles to work as a teacher. She had a brother, who was training to be a doctor in Manchester. He was the pride and joy of her parents, who ran a modest home and employed only one servant. Rose sent money every month, but probably not as much as she could afford, for which she felt guilty. I told her I didn't send money to my mum and she was surprised.

"Don't you provide for her as she provided for you?"

I told her that things were not the same in the UK, that education was free and that my mother and father had enough to live on without my help. I didn't mention that they were divorced. For some reason, I thought this might shock Rose too much. She wanted to know about Cambridge and Queens' College, where I had studied to be a teacher and she shook her head in disbelief when I told her that I had worked as a blackjack dealer for Playboy in London. I think she thought the job involved a more personal service than it actually did. As is the case in such situations, the more I assured her that it was nothing like that, the more she laughed and shook her head.

Eventually, we went inside, having watched a sunset partly obscured by clouds, but still awe-inspiring.

"Let's eat," said Rose. "But, first you might like a shower, and I have some wine."

I showered and got dressed, feeling quite hungry. Rose handed me a large glass of red wine as I came into the kitchen. She did not drink much and so, I didn't tell her that the wine was ghastly – sweet red wine was a new experience for me. The food, on the other hand, was delicious. We had chicken curry, so aromatic that I couldn't stop telling her how wonderful it was, until she told me to shut up. There was hot bread too, cooked directly over the gas flame like a chapatti. I can still taste the rich coconut sauce and the heat of the fresh chillies. In fact, the wine went well with the spicy food, in the end. Rose laughed and said that I would drink any wine. She obviously knew me too well.

We talked more, mostly about our home countries and what we intended to do in the future.

"You know that you could travel to Mauritius and stay with my mother and father?" she said, out of the blue. "They would be honoured to put you up and I could show you around, if you like. You and Carol, of course."

It was an offer too good to be missed. "That sounds amazing!"

There was a week's holiday coming up and I was sure that Carol would jump at the chance. I would ask her as soon as I got back.

"Thanks Rose."

It was getting on for eleven o'clock when Rose

said that she was tired. Not long after that, she was throwing up in the bathroom sink.

"Was it the curry?" I asked, only half joking.

"I think it was the fish I ate at lunch." She just managed to finish the sentence.

The basin was blocked. I wished that she had stuck her head down the rather basic toilet, instead. It was tempting to join in with the retching, and she waved me away gallantly.

I went back into the lounge, where my single bed suddenly seemed like the loneliest place on Earth and I wished I could be back at the house with Carol. Not only that, but my melancholy brought on that rushing feeling that makes you suddenly feel a sensation of enormous loss. The past came back to me in flashing images, carefree times, gone forever. Friends I had known, gone. Scattered to the four corners of the world.

Rose's eruptions died down and she came out smiling weakly. Purged and apologetic. We were both subdued and ready for bed, but there was a more worrying surprise awaiting me. Above my bed on the wall, was the most enormous spider I had ever seen.

"Oh, he won't hurt you," said Rose.

My horror was boundless.

"He has a girlfriend he visits. She lives behind the sideboard."

My heart very nearly stopped. I could not sleep in a room occupied by two gigantic, amorous spiders.

I managed to convince Rose that I was in fact not joking and that they would have to be evicted.

Before I knew it, she had fetched a broom and knocked the spider off the wall; it clambered off towards the sideboard. Rose pulled out the furniture and revealed its partner, at which point I could have died on the spot. I hoped she would catch them somehow and walk them to the other end of the beach.

She opened a cupboard and, just when I thought she was going to introduce the rest of the arachnid family, she took out a can of Doom and sprayed them for several seconds. Never have I felt so sorry and ashamed. I am certain they suffered and that they sought to defend each other. Rose then stamped on them in turn, mopped them up and put them in the kitchen dustbin.

I didn't sleep a wink. And even now, I am sure that if there is a purgatory, mine will be amongst these harmless creatures, bent on revenge for their violent and untimely destruction. Rose said it didn't matter and asked me whether I would like tea or coffee in the morning. We were separated by more than language and, for a moment, I didn't know whether I could bear it.

An Adventure in Mauritius

Carol and I had heard nothing about our resignation. She telephoned John and enquired whether a decision had been made. Nothing had been finalised, he said. He would follow it up, he promised.

So, we set our sights on the visit to Mauritius, which was planned for the half-term break, another British institution adopted by the NYS. Carol was raring to go and became very chummy with Rose during our brief voyages from the island to the mainland after work.

"Just pack some summer clothes. It will be very warm. It might rain at night, but not usually during the day."

"Can we travel around a bit?" asked Carol.

"My father will take us to visit the capital," replied Rose.

"What else is there to see?" I asked, wanting to join in the conversation.

"Oh, many places. Temples, shrines, museums. And beaches. Lots of beaches."

"Great."

"We can use bicycles to get around."

"That's good."

The conversation was not quite satisfactory. There was a gap between what we wanted to know and what Rose was telling us. She looked edgy at times, as though she were trying to hide something. I didn't realise at the time that she adored us, our western heritage and our shining future prospects. She wanted us to like her and to be impressed in some small way with the things she could offer us. She was a kind and sincere friend and I can picture her still, glowing with happiness, dreaming of shaking off the tethers that bound her and no doubt bind her still. Of course, it did not occur to me that she was proud of her way of life, just as we were of ours.

The last week at school was infused with the enthusiasm we had for our imminent adventure. The students told me all they knew about the island and dutifully warned me of the numerous dangers that lay in wait for a single woman travelling in a foreign country. I wondered whether they would ever have the same strong desire to travel and see the world as I had.

The end of the week arrived and we packed. Here we were, on the largest of the Seychelles islands, getting ready to jet off to yet another exotic location! Life was for living! We were blessed!

We flew out to Mauritius, looking out at the massive expanse of water below and making out the other islands on our path. Two thirds of the Earth is covered in water and it felt as though we were flying over the lion's share of it.

Rose's father, a small, wiry man with grey hair and high cheekbones met us in his astoundingly dilapidated car. He shook our hands and welcomed us, bowing a little and speaking to Rose in an altogether different tone, so that she grabbed our bags and put them in the boot. He spoke a little English, but relied on Rose to translate a lot of the time, wanting to know where in England we came from, telling us that his son was studying in Manchester, and wanting to know how far this place was from Cambridge or Devon.

It was dark outside, too dark to see anything but the lighted circle of road ahead. I had the feeling that there was something running along each side of the road, something tall and never-ending.

"It's sugar cane," said Rose, when I asked.

The idea that we had come to a place where sugar was actually grown was at first inspiring. However, we would soon learn that over eight per cent of the island was covered in this most lucrative of crops and that, as a result, there was rarely a view. It would be a bizarre sensation, never to see fields, trees or any open spaces as we travelled along roads without distinguishing features. I wondered what it had been like before, but it seemed that the plantations had been there since the arrival of the French.

Rose's mother was waiting for us. She was a feisty woman, a keen hostess and not afraid to give her husband the sharp edge of her tongue in front of guests. She referred to him, in a more or less ball-shrivelling, caustic tone, as 'le bonhomme Jagger' which, we came to learn, was a consequence of his ability to look into the future, as well as an ironic play on words.

"My mother is a teacher," Rose told us. "My father is retired." It was basic information, but the connotations were sticky and difficult to shake off. Her mother was still cogent, respected, vital; her father was ineffectual, past it and just a little barmy. In his defence, he did not put up a fight. He knew when he was beaten.

The house was low-ceilinged and gloomy, with curtains and tapestries draped everywhere. There was dark, solid-looking furniture and ancient, polished tiled floors. I don't know what I was expecting, but it felt homely, substantial. Our bedroom was on the ground floor, just off the dining room, and had a basin in a little alcove, in which we would wash, there being no shower, and the bath being for occasional use.

There was, about the house, a particular aroma. A mix of peppery spices and something that might be coffee. Rose took us out into the garden and showed us the coffee plant that grew there, its flowers fragrant.

"We have many things growing here. Herbs and vegetables. Fruit. My mother likes to be in the garden."

I got the impression early on that Rose's mother was a formidable woman. Not only did she work at the local school, but she also produced enough food to feed herself and her husband throughout the year, made everyone's clothes, and kept house to boot. What I did not find out immediately, was that the six-year-old girl whose elusive shadow I glimpsed from time to time, was a servant, employed full-time and expected to perform an implausible list of duties.

"What about school?" I asked Rose, discreetly.

"Oh, Celia doesn't go to school. Her parents can't afford it."

"What do you mean, can't afford it?"

"The schools here are not free," she said, smiling brightly. "Only those people who can pay can attend."

I was aware that this information was not entirely new to me, but its full impact hit me and must have shown on my face, for Rose shrugged her shoulders and said, "That's how it is. You and I are lucky."

I was lucky because I had received a free education and Rose was lucky because her parents had been able to pay for hers. We were all lucky in our different ways. Apart from Celia.

"Shit!" said Carol, later. "You mean that kid I saw in the kitchen is a slave?"

"Well, not exactly. The way Rose explained it was that the family is grateful for the money she earns. That this means they will have a better life."

Carol looked at me. Was I really beginning to think such an explanation reasonable? Did I want to justify the employment of a girl of six, who should be playing and going to infant's school to learn to read, paint pictures and play with Lego?

"Christ on a bike! The world's gone mad!"

She wasn't wrong.

Biking to the Beach

Like most inequalities in life, there are things you can change and things you can do nothing about. In fact, I have a quotation written down somewhere to that effect, copied into an old diary in a moment of weakness, which I won't bore you with now.

I rationalised the situation. We were visitors to another country, with an entirely different culture and a set of values accepted by the majority (naïve assumption). We would have to accept the status quo or get out. "Like it or lump it" the dinner ladies used to say at school, when I complained that I didn't like liver or big lumps of gristle. Well, I didn't like Mauritian ideas on education. Not one bit.

"I can take you to the beach, if you like," suggested Rose, over a breakfast of fruit and warm bread with tinned cheese, sliced thickly.

"Sounds good," we said.

"Take the bicycles," said her mother, "and I will make a packed lunch."

So it was that we set off on three very old but immaculately restored bikes (provided by her father) and, avoiding haphazard drivers, prolific potholes and the occasional crossing snake, we eventually came to a very plush hotel, similar to those found on Mahé. It was a bit of a disappointment, to be honest. It seemed as though we were in another third world country, scattered with super-rich tourists living in the lap of luxury, while children received an education if they were lucky enough to have the right kind of parents.

"We can go in," said Rose, oblivious to our political sensibilities.

We could go in. This meant Rose could go in with us. It was because we were with her. We looked like tourists. We had access to the bounty the hotel had on offer because we were foreigners.

We walked into Reception and through to the pillared quadrangle with its pool and Jacuzzi, firing on all cylinders. There wasn't a soul about. Further on, there was the beach, which Rose said was private. It looked the same as any other beach I'd seen in the Seychelles, that is to say, perfect, like a picture postcard of paradise. A few well-to-do sun worshippers lounged on the hotel's luxurious sunbeds or swam in the sea, their bodies generally toned and tanned. It felt surreal. As though we had stepped into an advertisement.

"Shall we sit under that tree for a while? Are you hungry?" said Rose.

There was a palm tree, almost horizontally parallel to the beach, casting an ideally sized shadow for three tired travellers. Rose took out three plastic bottles of lemon-mint tea that her mother had made and chilled for us and we were grateful for the refreshment.

"How much does it cost to stay here?" asked Carol.

"I'll go and find out," replied Rose, jumping up.

She grinned when we said not to bother, it

didn't really matter. But she went anyway.

"Would you like to stay here?" I asked Carol.

"Maybe. If it were with the right person."

"Who would that be?"

She picked up a handful of sand and let it run through her fingers. "Dave, I suppose."

It was no surprise that she had made this choice. Dave had been in her life for a very long time.

"Are you missing him?"

"A bit. Not really. It's just that, sooner or later, I have to make a decision."

"Why?"

"He wants to get married."

"He's always wanted to get married!" It was true. For the last seven years, Dave had been trying to get my beautiful pal to say yes.

"I know. But this time he means it. That's why I said I would come here."

"So you didn't actually break up, then?"

"It's a trial separation."

"That's a crappy name for it."

"I know. His idea. He was being sensible, he said. Practical."

"Is it helping?"

"Yes, and no."

She gave me a look that I remembered from years ago. We had spent three months in the south of France and were saying goodbye to the boys who had given us a lift to the train station. Carol had been the saddest I'd seen her. Sad to leave the boy she had fallen for. Sad that she would be leaving him behind and going back to

Dave. That had been her moment, her chance to break free.

Rose came back, beaming and brandishing a handful of leaflets. The hotel would be £120 per night for a double room, and remember, this was in the late eighties, which means it would probably cost in excess of a million, these days.

"Bugger me! That's a week's wages!"

Rose nodded, like one of those toys you put on the back shelf in your car, saying that it would keep her parents for a month. We laughed until we cried, to think of the absurdity of it all.

The picnic her mother had made for us consisted of sweet bread with more tinned cheese and some delicious roast vegetables with mango pickles. We chatted and watched the rippling waves, wondering whether to order a cocktail from one of the servers who was taking orders from a couple further down the beach, taking bets on how much it might cost for a bit of vodka mixed with pineapple juice and decorated with a paper umbrella.

"I need the loo," announced Carol.

"I'll show you where it is," offered Rose.

I lay back in the sand and stared up at the sun-lit fronds, clacking in the gentle breeze. I closed my eyes and thought of Sven. He got mixed up with the best aspects of all boyfriends past and brought a huge smile to my face. I was in mid reverie when I felt something tickle my head and looked up to see a woman, colourfully dressed, smiling down at me. I was disappointed, having hoped for a tall, semi-naked Swede to have materialised in paradise ready to whisk me into his arms.

"Bonjour, madame. Massage?" It was a basic introduction and a recognisable offer.

I sat up. "No, thank you."

The woman grinned and said, "Very good massage."

"I don't want a massage, thank you."

"No expensive." She was getting the measure of me.

It was tempting, but I didn't fancy being covered in the coconut oil she held out for inspection, and then inevitably pebble-dashed in sand. "Not today."

There was an awkward silence, during which one of us would have to make up our minds to give up and leave. I could see that it wasn't going to be her. I turned away slightly and tried to politely ignore her. Before I knew it, she had knelt down and started to massage my neck. Now, when I say that she was manipulating muscles that I didn't know I had, her deft fingers stunning me into submission, the pungent aroma of oils assaulting my senses, I am sure you will understand how helpless I was to protest.

It was only when I saw Rose running towards us, shouting something incomprehensibly Seychellois, that the friendly masseuse jumped up and, with a volley of what I presumed to be curses, fled, taking her fantastic fingers with her.

"They are shameless," said Rose. "They ask for too much money from the visitors. They have no education."

"I was enjoying that!" I wondered, simultaneously, at the irony of my friend's words.

Rose looked serious for a nanosecond and then grinned.

"Brilliant bogs here!" said Carol, saving the day, as usual. "Marble everywhere. Like a palace. I even sat down!" It was an impressive admission.

After relaxing unmolested for a while, due to Rose's ferocious treatment of the passing locals, who came to sell their wares and services, we decided we should get back before dark. We cycled through the village where Rose lived (I have tried, but I can't remember the name of it) where houses were sometimes makeshift and children playing in the street stared blankly. Rose and her family were well off. They had worked hard to get to the position they were in.

I didn't like Mauritius much, to begin with. As far as my very superficial knowledge went, it seemed to me that it was not striving towards a better social system, as the Seychelles was. There was an unacceptable division between the haves and the have-nots. This part of the world really was difficult to understand for a visitor like me.

Sightseeing, and a Gloomy Future

Rose's father had some business to see to in Port Louis, the capital, which lay in the north of the island. Rose lived in the south and the distance was a mere twenty miles or so, but it seemed to take forever as we trundled along, being overtaken by smoke-belching trucks and eventually stuck behind one of the slowest moving, filthiest vehicles I had ever seen. If you wanted to breathe, you kept the windows shut, in spite of the heat. Rose's father used his horn to little effect and eventually, as my fingernails dug into the seat, he lurched out onto the other side of the road and, engine screaming, laboured past, narrowly missing a truck coming in the opposite direction. He was not in the slightest bit alarmed, and continued his conversation without hesitation, informing us, via Rose, of the sightseeing opportunities in Port Louis.

We learned that the magnificent Government House was presided over by a statue of Queen Victoria, who was, apparently, sorely missed. The island had gained independence in 1968 but in 1987 the present Queen was still Head of State. We heard how the British had abolished slavery and forced the French plantation owners to give proper employment to workers. We Brits could do no wrong!

Rose interrupted him to tell us about the markets and the Botanical Gardens, which were the haunt of tourists by day and prostitutes by night. Her father tolerated this intrusion for a while and then got back to listing the various museums that we could visit – one of them contained a model of the very extinct dodo. Rose said it looked as though it had been made by a child. I have since seen pictures since, and have to agree with her assessment, a more likely candidate for extinction I have yet to see. We decided that we wanted to see the gardens, the markets and Government House.

Carol was sitting in the back with Rose and every now and then leaned forward to whisper in my ear, mostly praying and cursing, sometimes making personal comments about various parts of my body. It was funny, but I couldn't laugh, as le bonhomme Jagger spent more time looking at me than the road, and would have noticed.

It had rained the previous night and the tarmac shone in the gloom between the walls of sugarcane, which looked like bamboo. We had tasted the sugar, licking the inside of a cane and marvelling at the raw materials for the millions of sugar-based products the world had invented. The plant was a miracle, but it was a great pity that it grew so abundantly. It appears that, even now, nothing has changed; in fact today (if Internet statistics can be believed), eighty-five per cent of the island is given over to it.

I picture the solid ranks of cane and remember that during my sojourn in Mauritius they brought to mind (I have no idea why) Thérèse Desqueyroux's 'prison bars', which in turn, brought to mind the enthusiastic classes of a middle-aged French teacher who had once described to us how, in her younger days, she had been kissed by a very short Frenchman. The would-be suitor had stood on a chair in order to steal her heart. As she told the story, staring over our heads and into the past, the passionate encounter formed a sobering image in the mind of one of her students and, ever since, I have associated the slanting rain of the Landes and Thérèse's young face staring out of a window, with the image of a diminutive Frenchman reaching up to kiss the enraptured face of my softly spoken, forever unmarried French teacher. But I digress…

We arrived in Port Louis at a place that looked like a vast bus depot. It turned out that it was, in fact, a vast bus depot. There were hundreds of people criss-crossing the puddled tarmac and Rose said we should get out, join the throng, and explore the area on foot. First impressions? Port Louis was not a pretty place.

Rose's father rushed off with a flick of a wave, having promised that he would pick us up later. Unspecified meeting times were not a cause of concern for me in those days. Rather, I wondered where he would go and what he would do. Rose either didn't know, or didn't want to tell us so, as usual, I let my imagination run wild.

We headed for the centre – the capital was a small place, but very busy. The roads were generally narrow and one-way, bustling with traffic. We hit the markets and, compared to

Mahé, the diversity was overwhelming. It was just as colourful and noisy, but with more choice. The population was predominantly of Indian descent with a minority of Creole and various other ethnic groups, which were more or less in evidence at the market.

As always, we were drawn to the aroma of food. The market vendors sold chapattis cooked to order with a choice of spicy and sweet sauces, slathered on at lightning speed. The whole was then expertly rolled in paper and handed over. Rose took us to one that she deemed reputable and hygienic. The wraps were delicious.

"Blimey! I could eat about a dozen of these," said Carol.

So we did.

Next, we found Government House. It was a sight worth seeing.

"The French know a thing or two about architecture!" said Carol, gazing in at the out-of-bounds colonial style building.

"Very nice," I agreed. "Are we allowed in?"

"No," said Rose. "It's not open to the public."

"Top secret, I suppose," I said, picturing James Bond dropping down from the roof. Which James Bond, I hear you ask? Sean Connery, of course, I reply.

"Look who they've got on guard!" said Carol.

I scrutinised the famous statue of a very grumpy-looking Queen Victoria, which stood in front of the open-ended quadrangle.

"No need for a sign to keep people out," added

Carol, doing her best to emulate the 'we are not amused' look.

"What does the inscription say?"

Rose read it out: "To the memory of beloved and much regretted Queen Victoria Empress of India. The Inhabitants of Mauritius."

"Who's the chap at the back?" asked Carol, pointing out a bronze statue that we couldn't get to, and simultaneously bringing to mind a song by *The Sweet*.

"That's William Stevenson. He used to be the Governor of Mauritius," piped up our highly competent guide, a little too cheerfully.

"Never heard of him," replied Carol. "Only Stevenson I know is the one that invented the steam engine and that's because it was the only thing my Scottish history teacher ever taught us."

"I'm sure he was a very nice man," I said, soothingly.

"No he wasn't," said Carol, deliberately misunderstanding, "He had bad breath and an innate hatred of children."

Rose didn't understand or care about the nonsense we were amusing ourselves with. She was already looking at her watch.

We would visit the Botanical Gardens next, a short taxi ride away, in a place called Pamplemousse (Grapefruit). Rose assured us that the gardens were of a reasonable size and therefore not too daunting in the afternoon heat.

When we arrived, Carol spotted and fell under the charm of the baobab tree, which she tried to hug.

"It smells peppery," she said, stretching her arms out and looking as though she had splatted into it.

"It's huge!" I added.

Rose grinned and looked up through the tangled branches.

When we came to the water lilies, Carol was uncontrollable.

"Look at these buggers! Christ, you could get a family of four on one of those."

For a moment, I thought she was going to launch herself onto one and I cursed myself for not bringing a camera. Rose rushed forward with warnings coming out of every pore in her body, which made Carol laugh so much she nearly fell in the water anyway.

It was a beautiful place, with so many different types of palm that my over-loaded brain had no chance of remembering which were which. There was an avenue, regimentally planted and lovely, there were sausage trees and bottle palms. Carol was delighted, as much with the names as with the trees themselves.

"The gardens are over two hundred years old," Rose informed us.

"Blimey! Look at the size of those sausages! You wouldn't need many of those with your beans."

It was tiring wandering round in the afternoon heat and when we had had our fill of plant life we looked to Rose to rescue us. I was slightly disappointed not to be able to hang around until the streets were paved with prostitutes, but Carol said that we might be deemed to be unfair competition and have our eyes scratched out. In a rare moment of honest criticism, Rose said we were much too old, not beautiful enough and too bulky for Mauritian men.

We took her assessment of our charms on the chin and, after a refreshing drink of very sweet tropical squash, we retraced our steps and took a taxi back to the centre, half listening to Rose's running commentary, hoping that her father would be waiting, and sober.

The journey back was even more death-defying than the outward one, as the light was failing and the single working headlight glimmered weakly. We passed a couple of trucks with no lights at all, huge rumbling shadows hurtling towards us. Le bonhomme Jagger, oblivious to our fear, held on to the steering wheel with one hand and searched for a suitable radio station with the other. Having rejected *Those Magnificent Men in their Flying Machines*, he settled on some rousing classical music by Beethoven, and I composed a beautiful prayer inside my head to my favourite saint, who happened to be Saint Christopher, knowing that if disaster struck, the only word that I would have time to utter would probably be *fuck*!

By some miracle, we were not killed. Drained of blood and numb to the world, but not dead.

Rose's mum had prepared a fantastic feast of fritters, curried fish and sticky rice so we gradually came round as we tucked in and related the events of the day, leaving out the boring bits and elaborating on the interesting ones. We drank a local brew, similar to the toddy made in Seychelles, and the evening quietly gave way to tipsy hilarity. Carol became her usual serious self after a while. It was impossible to imagine that she was in the first stages of alcohol poisoning as she began to quiz our bemused hosts with an unnerving level of sobriety.

"What do Mauritians dream about?" she said, fixing first Rose and then each of her parents.

"That's an interesting question," replied Rose's mum.

It was obvious only to me that Carol had instantly forgotten what she had asked.

"I think a man must have a hobby," added le bonhomme Jagger.

This was too much for his wife. "Ah! A hobby… Yes, of course. A hobby!" Old wounds opened and unspoken contempt hovered like evil spirits.

Carol had another question: "Why do people call you *bonhomme*?"

Whilst I was not in the least surprised at this indiscretion, our Mauritian host shifted in his seat and did well to maintain a pleasant expression of enforced tolerance.

"It denotes a connection with another dimension." Le bonhomme said, enigmatically.

"Pah!" Rose's mum got up and went out of the room.

Carol had closed her eyes, so I took over. "Another dimension?" (It was all in the inflection

-
151
-

– you had to be there.)

"I see what others do not."

"I see." (I didn't.)

"Things that lie behind the veil of the present."

"The veil?"

"What he means," said Rose's mum, who had come back unexpectedly, "is that he reads fortunes!"

There followed a brief husband and wife altercation in the local language, during which, Carol snorted and woke up.

"Rose's dad reads fortunes," I told her.

With eyes wider than a child's at Christmas, Carol stuck out her hand and said, "Me first."

"It's done with tea leaves," said Rose.

Magically, the tea appeared before us. Green. Floating. We stirred it, drank it and followed the instructions we were given, finally swirling the small amount of tea around the cup three times and tipping out the dribble of liquid into the saucer. Carol handed her cup over.

"You will marry."

"Who will I marry?" she slurred.

"A man of the earth."

"Not Dave!"

"And have seven children."

"Fuck off!"

(Here, there was a short hiatus.)

"You will be rich."

"That's better!"

"But you will suffer a terrible illness."

"Eh?"

"I can tell you no more."

Next, it was my turn. I pushed my cup forward, not altogether enthusiastically.

"Ah!"

"What?"

"Oh!"

"What is it!"

"You will die young!"

I was already approaching thirty.

"On an aeroplane. A man. There is a gun. Bang!"

"Shit!"

"I can tell you no more."

Having revealed our wretched futures, it was more or less time for bed. Rose told us not to worry about it, that he was sometimes wrong. Her mother told us he was an imbecile and a fraud.

Carol and I climbed into bed and, as I listened to the onset of her snufflings, I tried not to obsess too much about what the odds were of being taken down, or out, or whatever people say in films, on a Boeing 747.

Sebastian's Coconut Skills

We were back! The house was full of insects, mostly ants, and there was an overwhelming stench of dead lizard coming from the toilet.

"Dozy bastards," muttered Carol.

"Will it flush?"

It wouldn't.

We had flown back on a Saturday and it was a wonderfully comforting feeling to know that the next day would be given over to relaxing and regrouping before the return to Ste. Anne and a renewed attempt to do something useful in the classroom.

"How long have we been here now?"

"Not quite long enough," replied Carol, in a Mary Poppins moment.

"I wonder whether John has sorted out our return tickets yet?" I mused, putting to the back of my mind the painful realisation that our time together would soon come to an end.

"Not a chance! Things don't happen in the Seychelles." I knew what she meant; she hadn't just forgotten the adverb.

There was a postcard from Marc:

You should come! Weather great. Boat to La Digue nearly sank! Turtles all around. Caught wahoo and roasted on beach. Praslin house needs you! Bisous, Marc

"Shall we go next time?" I wondered out loud.

"Should do, really," replied Carol, "Not much time left, now."

"Are you going to marry him, then?"

Carol didn't need me to tell her that I was talking about Dave, not Marc.

"Christ knows. Probably," she said. "But not tonight! Let's get pissed! Sort out the music, you gorgeous bugger!"

The cheap imported South African rum was rough, but when mixed with juice, was passable. We had ice, the stars, Bananarama, and an evening to wile away with philosophical blatherings and unrealistic plans for the future.

Carol was tanned, and glowed with health and happiness in the lamplight. She talked about Dave with affection, if not passion, while I remembered him from years ago and pictured them together, growing old and relying on one another for all that was essential. We both knew that there would be something missing. A spark, a longed for moment of unpredictability. A niggling question mark that would occasionally rankle, but as we grew older, we were learning to accept this shortfall and I was even curious about what came next, after the first glorious years of getting to know someone. There must be surprises along the way, mustn't there?

"What about you?" Carol sat back in her chair, her nostrils flaring in the night air.

"Still looking for Mr. Right," I said, laughing at the cliché, picturing Sting, and taking an enormous swig of my evil drink.

"Overrated."

It was clear once more that the problem lay and would always lie in the old adage about the grass being greener on the other side. Would I ever find someone I could be happy with? The evening wore on in an increasingly powerful haze as the Icebreaker numbed our brains and made us sentimental.

"Don't worry, *I'll* always love you!" I slurred, as Carol tucked me up in my bed.

She wiped away the dribble from my chin and put a finger to her lips. "Get some sleep, you lovely dullard," she murmured, kissing me on the forehead.

"I wish *I* could marry you! Do you love me as much as I love you?" I wailed, overcome by the random truths I was airing.

I didn't register her answer. Perhaps I had fallen asleep instantly, or perhaps she had not spoken. Either way, it was enough to believe that she felt the same way as I did.

The next day began at two o'clock in the afternoon, with the arrival of Sebastian, a Seychellois Carol had met at the bus stop a few days before our trip to Mauritius.

"Wakey, wakey," she said, "Sebastian's here."

By the time this information had circled the area of my brain that was still functioning, and made me scowl, Carol had gone, leaving me wondering who Sebastian was and why he was in our house. I stared at the ceiling and listened to the conversation that seemed to be taking place on the balcony. I turned over, muttering to myself, and dozed off again.

"Toast," said Carol, "and coffee?"

I stirred, sniffing the air, hearing the clatter of plates in the kitchen. Moving carefully, I slipped on my pink robe, not bothering to do it up, and noticing that my hair had once more transformed into a lopsided bird's nest structure and my mascara had migrated south, forming shadowy rifts and fractures in my otherwise grey complexion, I wandered out and came face to face with a very tall, very slim, very shiny man.

"Good morning!" said Sebastian, his startlingly white teeth filling my world. I was Alice and he was the Cheshire Cat.

My hands fumbled with the belt of my gown and I could utter no comprehensible response, grunting in what I hoped was an apologetic way. As I did a sweep for Carol, Sebastian continued to be cheerful, while I continued to wish that he were not there.

"Seb has brought some coconuts and a bottle of homemade toddy," said Carol, from the kitchen, loudly enough to hurt my head. I was petulant by this time and ready to dislike any offering put before me.

Seb laughed. It was a nasal, high-pitched squeak of a laugh, tooth-rich and eye-bright. His presence in our tranquil home offended me on so many levels that I still could not speak.

"Will you show us how to open one?" said Carol coming out of the kitchen looking immaculately groomed. How was this possible?

"No problem. I can do it anytime. Anytime you like it." Seb slid out onto the balcony and down the steps.

"What's he doing here?" I hissed, clutching the side of my head, where an invisible knife was reminding me of how much I had drunk the night before.

"You look awful," replied Carol. "Why don't you drink this and then have a shower?"

There was no reason to doubt her advice. In fact, it was wonderful to have someone tell me what to do, so that I could stop thinking altogether. But, as was usual when I felt so hung-over, it was difficult not to suspect anyone else who appeared so immune to the consequences of alcohol.

"Why do you look so normal?"

"That's one of the nicest things you've ever said to me!" beamed my buddy.

"But, what's going on?" I whined.

"Nothing. Just go and get dressed. You think too much!"

A variety of conspiracy theories assaulted my tangled brain. Perhaps Sebastian had given Carol a happy pill, perhaps he was waiting for me to drink my drugged coffee. We would be bundled into the back of a Mini Moke and shipped to a land where men longed for synthetic creations from the west.

"Shoo!" said Carol. Carol never said *shoo*. I didn't budge. "Bugger off, you silly cow! Stop gawping like a birdbrain!" That was more like it.

I was reassured. Life was simple, after all. Why complicate it?

So, after I had rinsed off, sorted out my face and my hair, spilled my coffee over the bedroom floor and mopped it up with a pair of knickers, I returned, slightly less bumptious, to find the house deserted. Carol and Seb were in the garden under the balcony, waiting for me, and ready to sort out some coconuts. I went down, too curious to resist, and saw Carol standing next to one of our dining-room chairs, with Seb indicating a long stick, sunk upright into the ground, anchored against a rock, poised for Carol to bring down a coconut onto its pointed end. Seb laughed and Carol cursed.

"Christ! This is impossible!"

Seb beckoned for her to lift the coconut higher and, after she had had a couple more determined attempts, she threw the unopened coconut to the ground and he took over, removing the hairy skin in less than a minute, making a hole in the top with his pocket knife and handing it to Carol, gesturing for her to drink.

"It's sweet," she said, handing it to me.

It was sweet and warm, watery and thin. I didn't have to pretend that I didn't like it.

"You can make cream – it tastes better," suggested the indomitable nutcracker.

Carol fetched a bowl and our jovial guest found a flattish rock, which he placed on the chair and sat on, legs akimbo, pushing the halved coconut down rhythmically onto the end of the rock that protruded over the bowl. It cost him dear, I think, as the rock was irregular and not the right tool for the job. The coconut meat looked dry, but after wrapping it in a pair of Carol's tights and squeezing, the creamy milk was collected in the other half of the nut. And it was delicious!

"Thank you, Seb," I said, genuinely amazed by this new delicacy.

"You are welcome," he beamed.

Our friendly new acquaintance stayed for a while and told us that he was looking for work. He wanted to be a bus driver, but competition for such an important job was tough. In the meantime, he fished and took his catch to the market, like many of the men on the island.

But Seb was young and had ambition. He had seven brothers and two sisters, all younger than him. His father visited seldom and so he was the main breadwinner for the time being. His mother worked as a seamstress and sold small touristic articles at the market from time to time.

"What a nice bloke," said Carol, after he had left.

It was true. He was a man with a plan that was simple and, with luck and enthusiasm, attainable. It was strange that he never visited a second time and I hoped that I had done nothing to offend him. Whenever I do remember him, he is smiling broadly or laughing, young and ready to take on the world. I pictured the bus driver in Cambridge who had once closed the doors on me while I waited for my mother to arrive. I couldn't imagine Seb doing anything like that.

"Maybe he got run over by a bus," suggested Carol.

"Maybe his mother forbade him to visit the harlots on the hill, ever again," I countered.

"Speak for yourself, you old scrubber!"

"Hah! Want a cuppa, my lovely Devonshire strumpet?"

"And toast?"

"Let's party!"

New Year at Anka's

It was coming up to Christmas and the French contingent was going home, all flights paid for, courtesy of the French government. Rose was joining her family too, in Mauritius. She had invited us, but we didn't want to intrude and, to be honest, we felt that we might be bored (and boring) the second time around. I had always been taught not to outstay my welcome. Three nights was the limit, my grandmother had always told me, then people started to show their real character! God forbid! So, we would be left on our own, apart from Penny and Dick, who had come up with the less than alluring suggestion that we celebrate together at the beach in Beau Vallon. Carol said that she would rather have all my fingernails pulled out.

"Don't you mean *your* fingernails?"

"No."

"Maybe we should give them a chance?" I suggested, with a startling measure of sincerity that took Carol aback for a second.

"I'd rather you dived naked, into a pool of stone fish!" replied Carol.

Stonefish are lethal, but apparently not as lethal as the company of Penny and Dick. Thank God for Carol's no-bones-about-it principles.

We were united in our terror of Penny and her drip of a husband, and politely refused their kind invitation (shame and ingratitude lasted a teeny-weeny moment). Then, we set about organising our own entertainment by baking our individual version of a Christmas cake (chocolate instead of marzipan, fresh fruit instead of dried), making a Christmas pudding (Icebreaker instead of brandy), meringues (flat – no electric whisk), a new version of sherry trifle (more sherry than trifle and coconut milk instead of custard), and by getting some cheap lights and decorations to brighten up the balcony and lounge.

On Christmas Eve, there would be a midnight mass in Mahé at the Roman Catholic church. These days, I would have gone like a shot, but then I was rather prone to idleness and couldn't be bothered. Church? Boring! Plus, I couldn't sing and wouldn't pray. So, instead, we tootled down to the beach in the afternoon and relaxed with our books, borrowed from the small library provided by the British High Commission (thank you very much). It was bliss, but the early sunset made our time short, and brought back memories of killer sand flies.

Soon, we were back at the house decorating ourselves with tinsel and getting stuck into some festive booze we had discovered at the local shop. It was sweet and tasted like Tia Maria mixed with gravy browning. Carol, in experimental mood, combined it with UHT milk, put it in coffee, mixed it with mango juice and finally declared that it was undrinkable. She would never touch another drop! It was the last bottle standing until much later that evening, when resolve weakened and we finished most of it off with a bowl of creepy-crawly cereals, having hilarious fun making up squeaky weevil conversations.

When we had committed this final act of folly, we both felt like throwing up, as you can imagine. The room rotated, making me laugh uncontrollably. My feet were no longer mine to command, and I navigated haphazardly, pinging off the walls, towards the bathroom. Carol had a knack for putting her fingers down her throat, but I laboured long and hard in vain, failing to divest myself of my poisonous belly full of booze, finally flopping into a chair and going to sleep in the early hours of Christmas morning. Carol stayed up and ate an enormous piece of Christmas cake, which, she said, had settled her stomach nicely. Why did we do it? Your guess is as good as mine. The person that was Bev at thirty is an exotic and inscrutable puzzle to me now. I am grateful to her for not accidentally putting an end to herself with her occasional bouts of excess, and even more thankful for the adventures she went on so that I can recount some of them here. (The author pours herself a second litre of curative green tea.)

Christmas was, to all intents and purposes, a non-event. We ate too much, drank too much, didn't go to Victoria, didn't go down to the beach to see if there was a party going on and gradually sank into a second stupor. At our age, it was getting to be hard work.

We were gradually going stir crazy, resorting to *I Spy with my Little Eye*.

"I spy with my little eye, something beginning

with 's'," I said.

"Sun?"

"No."

"Socks?"

"No."

"Spider?"

"Where!"

"Hah!"

"I hate you!"

"Well?"

"No!"

"What is it, then?"

"Do you give up?"

"Clue, please."

"It's big, lumpy and pickled." I could hardly keep a straight face.

Carol was on to me.

"Do you want to know?" I giggled.

Carol sighed.

"Shall I tell you?"

"You are insufferable."

I started to hyperventilate.

"Tell me! I know it's going to be stupid, but just tell me!"

"It's *spaz*!"

"Oh, ha flippin' ha! Excuse me while I re-arrange my ribs."

"Don't get tetchy, just because you lost… Your turn, now."

"You do know that you are a much bigger spaz than me, don't you?" said Carol, a little smugly, despite her sound intellectual beating.

"So, what you are saying," I crowed, "is that I

am, to all intents and purposes, a spaz with knobs on?"

"Times infinity." She drew a symbol in the air to represent the number without end.

I was unable to continue our discussion, as there was a knock at the door. It was Anka. She was passing and wanted to invite us to come over for New Year's Eve. She was having a few guests and there would be a barbeque on the beach. I hugged her and dragged her inside. She said that she had been awarded another grant to continue her work, and that Dragan was divorcing her. We made coffee and listened, not knowing which news she considered to be the most exciting.

We arrived for the barbeque kitted out in our most alluring attire and carefully made up. We had ambitiously decided not to drink too much and not to stay too late. It was reassuring to see some old faces and thrilling to be out of our island retreat. Not everyone had gone home, it seemed, or if they had, they had returned to celebrate the New Year in paradise.

Marc was there and so were Sven and Marianne. My stomach gave an involuntary lurch and my nipples tingled very naughtily. Carol deserted me immediately and went to talk to Marc. I hung around in the kitchen with Anka for a while, who had made it up with Dragan (apparently, deciding to get divorced was a regular event), and then was commandeered to go and look at their daughter, Lou's, collection of stamps. I listened and looked and she held onto my hand whenever I made a move to leave. The stamps were lovely, very colourful, and I told her so. She had fixed them very neatly, I was impressed. How old was she? What? Only eight! It was incredible. She liked all of this and kept me to herself for the best part of half an hour, by which time I had reneged on my promise to myself to stay away from alcohol, and resorted to staring at the door, behind which lay freedom and bottles of intoxicating liquor. At last, Anka popped her head round, and I slid out.

"Happy Christmas!" I looked up from pouring a large glass of wine, to see Sven and his wolf smile.

"Where's Marianne?" I replied, attempting to raise an eyebrow and remembering that this was always the question I asked first when I saw Sven.

"She's over there."

She was nearby, and her passivity in the face of danger was unnerving.

"Shall we go for a walk?" he asked, putting down his glass and taking my hand.

"But… What?" I was unused to such overt dishonesty. In fact, I had never knowingly two-timed anyone outside the boundaries of the Indian Ocean.

He put a finger to his lips to shush me. "Come. It's okay."

I did my very best not to look at Marianne, and followed Sven out into the garden, which dropped steeply away towards the beach. He led me to some steps and I staggered down behind him, all the time telling myself that this was a very bad idea. The stars were amazing, as usual, so many and so bright. He was amazing. I was in love with the back of his head and wanted to stroke his gorgeous yellow hair.

"Where are we going?" I murmured.

He stopped and turned. "Here," he said, closing in for a kiss.

"Just a…" I made a pathetic effort to stop him.

"Relax."

Relax? That did it! I remembered a boy with the unlikely name of Bo Bo telling me the same thing as he sat with me on a bench on the banks of the River Severn many, many years ago. I didn't like his patronising tone then and I didn't like Sven's now. I felt my hackles rising (did you know that 'hackles' are the hairs on the back of a dog's neck? I didn't), and I bristled with indignation. What utter crap!

"Stop! Who the hell do you think you are? You have a fiancée inside and you're behaving like a moron! Is it because you are stupid, or just that you believe yourself to be irresistible?" I looked into his eyes and my knees buckled.

He laughed. He actually laughed! I regained my balance and shook him off. I felt like Sophia Lauren, venomous against the outrageous advances of a handsome stranger. I stuck out my chest and raised my chin. I almost stamped my foot. Then, I stamped my foot.

Sven took out a cigarette and lit up. He looked so handsome that I very nearly swooned again, and pictured myself gently falling into his arms (could he support ten stones?), awaking to find him cradling my head and stoking my hair.

Oh, Sven! I would murmur. *Oh, oh, Sven, darling*!

"Oi! Tartface! What the fuck are you doing down there with that cretin? Get your arse away from him and come up for some dancing fun."

"Carol!" I screamed, and ran up the steps, leaving Don Juan to contemplate the night alone and to consider the questionable morality of his sordid existence.

Anka said that Dragan had gone down to the beach with some others and was setting up the barbeque. In the meantime, she excused herself and went out into the night with the man I had seen her kissing at the party we had attended several weeks previously. I wondered whether the whole world had gone mad. Hadn't she told me that the divorce was off? That Dragan and she were back on?

My attention was drawn to a quiet mewling close by. Marianne was crying in the corner and Carol was hugging her. Sven was nowhere to be seen. This was expat life, then. Surely not everyone could be up to no good? I went down to the garden again for some fresh air and nearly fell over Sven and a girl I'd never met before, at a very advanced stage of introduction.

"Hi, Bev. Want to join us?"

"Argh!"

"Shall we go home?" I said, hovering as close as I dared to my bosom buddy and her blubbing companion.

"Won't be long. Could you fetch some tissues?"

I found some kitchen roll and a man who said he was a local friend of the family stacking beer into a bag, presumably to take down to the beach. He seemed very friendly, asking whether there was any other alcohol in the house. I showed him the cupboard where the spirits were kept.

"Don't you want some fish?" said Marc, as Carol and I collected our helmets and headed outside.

"Not really," I said. The evening was more or less ruined, as far as I was concerned.

"Bit too much for her." Carol winked at Marc.

"What?" I protested.

"Nothing." Carol saved me from falling over backwards.

"Not everyone is the same as Sven," said Marc, lecherously.

"Right," I replied. "See you later." What did *he* know!

After he had gone inside, Carol tapped on my helmet and mouthed, "Marc's all right."

Christ! I thought. *Not you too*!

"Some bastard's nicked all the booze!" shrieked Anka, running out of the house and looking frantically up and down the road.

The drive home was beautiful, if hazardous. There were parties going on all along the beach, spilling onto the road. We stopped a few times just to watch the fires, the boats on the water and the children scudding in the sand. I thought of fairytales and magic. Carol said she was being eaten alive by insects and needed a poo.

At home, I put the bike in the garage and Carol nipped in with a camera. "Smile," she said. I still have the photo – me in a white strapless dress bought from Monsoon in Cambridge, for a May ball I never made it to on account of the wall being too high, and a helmet lined with dead ants, bought from a man halfway up a hill on the outskirts of Mahé.

"It's just gone midnight," said Carol. "Have we got any bog roll?"

"In the cupboard under the sink."

"Happy New Year you tart, by the flippin' way!" Carol fled, squealing, towards the bathroom.

"Happy New Year, my best friend in all the world," I murmured.

A Bus Journey to Hell

It was time to get heavy with the authorities.

I made an appointment to see John and, when we arrived, there was a second person in the room, a representative of the NYS whom we had not met before. He was there to observe, we were told.

The conversation was brief. We were expected to fulfil our contract, which we had agreed to and signed. There were no mitigating circumstances and therefore, no obligation on the part of the Seychelles authorities to concede to our wishes. It all seemed quite straightforward – Carol and I would have to take our case to the Embassy and enlist support. We seethed with the injustice of it all and were about to leave, when the mysterious gentleman in the corner of the room cleared his throat and came forward. He had in his hand, copies of our qualifications and he wore on his face a benevolent smile.

"We are not unsympathetic," he began. "It is unfortunate that you are not satisfied with your terms of employment." He paused, but it was obvious that there was more. "The NYS would like to suggest a change to your duties," he continued.

I wondered whether we were to be put in charge of toilet cleaning and issued with loo brushes and buckets. Punished for daring to rebel.

"Your qualifications are impressive. As you

know, materials are scarce on Ste. Anne. We have few books." He held out his hands and I noted that they were indeed empty. "It is with great pleasure that I offer you the opportunity to design and produce materials for years one and two. If you are agreeable, of course."

It was true that we had been vocal in our criticism of the inadequate teaching materials and, to some extent, the less than stimulating methods used by a few of the teachers. This would be our challenge, then. To put our money where our mouth was and create a better curriculum, to raise the level of interest and provide suitable input in the classroom. All the theory I had laboured over at Queens' College and later at The Bell School of English would at last be put to proper use. It was an offer I knew I could not refuse.

"Can we let you know after the weekend?" asked Carol.

"Of course," replied the man who had not introduced himself. "I will leave John to sort out the details with you." He held out a hand and said that it had been a pleasure. Carol held open the door and grunted.

We waited for the bus back to Anse à la Mouche (we did not travel to work by motorbike as it would ruin our hair, and involved fuel costs), considering the brand new situation.

"I like the sound of it," I admitted.

"Me too," agreed Carol. "But we still have to leave. Nothing has changed. We're still skint and not allowed to travel outside the islands or Mauritius."

It was true.

"How come we are allowed to go to Mauritius, anyway?" It was a question I'd been thinking about for a while.

"Marc told me that it was originally part of the Seychelles group and was given its independence when the Brits took over from the French, about two hundred years ago. Then the Seychelles became an independent republic, but stayed in the Commonwealth. I suppose the original connections make a difference."

"Fancy!" It was a far more comprehensive answer than I'd been expecting.

Carol moved seamlessly on. "I think we should accept the new work – they obviously need us – but aim towards leaving after a couple more months. We'll go and see the High Commissioner and ask whether he can support us. Deal?"

"Spot on, Miss Baker. Good plan!" I put my arm through Carol's and glowed with the awe I felt for my wonderful level-headed buddy.

The bus arrived and there was much pushing and shoving. It was not the usual teachers' transport, but a public service. After a chaotic boarding, amongst the usual chickens and babies and the rather new sacks of bread and pots of what smelled like fish soup, the driver, who was almost too large for his cab, started a conversation with an old woman sitting behind us. We were unsurprised, having become immune to such informalities during our roller coaster introduction to Seychelles life.

We took the main road out of town to start with, blissfully ignorant of the knicker-filling adventure that was to follow, marvelling at the driver's jolly demeanour and the woman's constant flow of conversation. I understood a lot of the words, but the meanings of the utterances as a whole were mostly unfathomable.

Carol stuck her arm through mine and grinned. "Great here, isn't it?"

"Wonderfully mad," I replied, looking forward to getting home and eating the curry we had left over, with some fresh bread and pickle.

About half way home, the bus swerved extravagantly and a cry went up. All at once, we were climbing a steep, narrow road, looking out at an increasingly sheer drop to the side we were sitting on. Neither of us could speak, except to mutter a series of predictable curse words under our breath.

The driver paid minimal attention to the road, preferring to comment on the now vociferous reactions of the other passengers. It became obvious that there was a majority of travellers who had not agreed to this detour up the mountain, which, it seemed, had been instigated by the woman behind us. We turned around and she grinned – her two front teeth having presumably been taken out during a previous bus journey involving an emergency stop.

The bending road continued until, stopping at what looked like a wooden shack, the driver shouted to the woman, who descended with two others, paid over an undisclosed sum of rupees to the driver at his cab window, and delivered a number of sacks of bread, vegetables, live chickens and pots of fish soup to a man and his son, who came over to the bus and chatted with the driver, who was hanging out of the window ready to accept a further greasing of his palm.

"Fuck! I don't like this," said Carol. "Shall we get off and take our chances walking?"

"But where are we?"

"Not a clue. But if we stay on this death wagon, we're going to end up at the bottom of the mountain with our brains smashed out!"

We had seen a number of people without any front teeth walking around Victoria and the story went that there had been a routine accident, throwing the passengers forward onto the metal bars that topped the seats. The metal bars that Carol and I were hanging on to for dear life. We had not yet heard of any deaths *en masse* in public transport plummets, however, we did not read the newspapers and for all we knew such events could be a weekly occurrence. Perhaps that was one of the reasons for the stagnant growth in ethnic population. Bus drivers were killing people off!

"Yeah, let's get out," I said.

But it was too late. The drop had been made and the motley passengers, drug dealers and gun runners (for all we knew), smuggling their wares inside chickens and soup, re-boarded with a swagger or two, sending out a few half-comprehensible invectives to those who dared question their hijacking tactics. All rants were cut short, however, as those still standing staggered hilariously when the fun-loving driver released the handbrake.

I think Carol and I screamed the loudest, as the bus began reversing, jolting us in our seats, making our stomachs swarm, and activating various other basic physiological reactions with a dose of primeval terror. I looked around, wondering what was happening. With the part of my brain that had not gone into shock I reasoned that, surely, we would not retrace our steps in reverse! Then, the vehicle began to rise, backwards, up a track so steep that the roar of the engine threatened to burst my eardrums, I do not exaggerate. The bus lurched and stopped as the driver turned the steering wheel and endeavoured to keep the tyres in contact with the road.

We were turning round on a road meant only for goats. People laughed. People cooed and gasped, as if they were at a circus, watching daring feats designed to thrill. This was all very well, but did they realise that here, there were no safety nets? I looked out of the window and saw that the front of the bus was hanging over the edge of the road. Remember *The Italian Job*? That was us, in reverse, except that, somehow, the wheels skirted the edge of the road and, at an unimaginable angle, we came to rest for a moment, after a second round of reversing, poised at the T junction of life and death.

The view was terrifying. Down we came, praying that there would be enough road to make the turn. Staring with a newfound love and affection at our terrorist driver, dependent hostages, willing him to do a good job. Inching forward and sticking it into reverse a couple more times, the bus eventually tilted alarmingly onto the road and, miraculously undead, in body if not in spirit, we commenced our descent, back to the main coastal road.

"Fuck a duck!" murmured Carol.

I clutched my friend's hand. "I think I might need a change of pants," I said. And it turned out, when we got home, shaken but in one piece, that I did.

A New Challenge

The next time we saw our regular driver, I almost kissed him. Almost.

We had told Rose that we would not be teaching any longer and she had cried. She would see us again, we said, at parties and at our house. We would come to Beau Vallon for a visit. Not to worry.

She told us that her house had been broken into for the second time and some of her things had been stolen. The thieves had removed the louvre glass slats from the window while she slept and climbed silently in. They had taken her cassette player, her jewellery and her purse, which contained the rupees she had taken out for the week ahead.

"Do you have insurance?" I asked. Speaking before thinking, as was my wont.

"No. Do you?"

"No."

The most worrying aspect of the robbery, in my opinion, was that some of the things that the thieves had taken, had been on Rose's bedside table. But this didn't seem to bother her as much as the losses she had suffered.

"Didn't you hear anything?" asked Carol.

"Nothing," replied Rose. "They even put the slats back in the window when they left."

I pondered the baffling notion of such polite pilferers.

On the morning of our first day at the office, the bus dropped us off at the NYS building and John showed us the resources that would be at our disposal. There was a pc, with plug and electric socket, no Internet of course, various outdated textbooks, one or two of which were familiar to us, unlimited paper, some staples the wrong size for the stapler, and some scissors. We set to work. Carol had the ideas and I had the formal training. Carol could spell and I could type. We made a great team.

We wanted to create useable booklets, with adequate materials to last a term. Three of them for each year. It was ambitious but engrossing, and soon we had chosen extracts and created suggested questions and activities to go with them. We even created a teachers' booklet, organising the pages to be simple to use. On one side, we set out the students' materials and activities and on the other, a simple lesson plan for the teachers to refer to if they wished. It was practical, thorough and crucially, fun. Unfortunately, there would be negative responses from some of the teachers to all three of these criteria. It must have been very difficult for our fellow professionals to take seriously anything produced by two brightly coloured foreigners who believed themselves to be at the cutting edge of modern educational methods.

At lunchtimes, we generally went to a wooden roadside shack opposite, and bought spicy burgers and slices of *gateau piment* for lunch, the latter being a kind of chilli Spanish omelette. It was a change from the fish and rice we had eaten nearly every day on Ste. Anne. In the sunshine, sitting on the steps outside the offices, with the wooded slopes of the island in view, I was happy, and I think Carol was too. Our work drove us on and we were absorbed throughout the day, creating the booklets that would be used by the National Youth Service, as the main teaching resource for both schools on the island of Ste. Anne. It was an honour and a joy to have such a challenge.

Once completed, the first term's work for each year was ready for copying and submission to the relevant authorities for approval. It was with a naïve sense of pride that we knocked on the door to the secretary's office and enquired politely whether she would make copies, which we would then bind, to be presented to John, her boss.

Millicent's expression, when she found the energy to turn and acknowledge our presence, was blank. There was no enthusiasm behind her pleasant, cow eyes. The only busy thing about her was the floral pattern on her dress. She plonked the precious folder, our life's work over the past three weeks, into a tray filled with dog-eared, crumpled papers. We would have to wait, she said, until she had time to do the work. Little did we know that 'time' to Millicent, was rarely filled with doing anything at all, least of all work.

"What was she staring at when we came in?" I asked Carol.

"The wall," she replied.

"Thought so."

Millicent must live in a world of her own, I concluded. (Being a person who was generally found inhabiting a variety of invented universes, I could not help being curious about the version of Millicent that we could not see.)

Undaunted, Carol and I returned to our task of preparing the second term's materials. Having got into our stride, the second and third would be easier. Ideas flowed, and my touch typing skills were a boon. Two weeks later, Millicent still had not copied the contents of the first folder, which had moved, in a direct assault on logic, to the bottom of the in-tray. I wondered whether the next move would be into the rubbish bin, which was overflowing, and I began to panic.

I mentioned the hold up to John and, by the next afternoon, the copying had been done. We thought we should check it. The pages had not been collated and half of them were crooked or partly missing. Marxist Millicent had exercised her right to be a pain in the arse, and, when challenged about her sloppy work, was predictably unsorry. It was time to grab the bull by the horns, charge with it into her office and take control of the photocopy machine. I muscled past her, noticing one of the strongest body odours I'd ever come across, while Carol set to work with the ancient photocopier. We did what we needed to do and Millicent ignored us. In the end, the absurdity of it all made us giggle like schoolgirls and Millicent thawed a little, showing us her real self for a moment, and leading to a generous offer of some undrinkably sweet tea.

John was delighted, and the materials were sent off to be properly printed and bound. It was a seminal moment in our humble careers. In print, in the Seychelles. As far as we knew, our fame would not spread beyond the Indian Ocean. But that didn't matter. Not a jot. A little piece of Seychelles would be forever England! (Sorry, couldn't resist.)

There was only one more term's materials to be created, when we received a message from the High Commissioner, whom we had called to ask for a rendezvous and promptly forgotten about the whole thing. So, it was with great surprise that we read the hand-written, genteel invitation to tea and cakes at his residence in Victoria.

The motorbike trundled up the rise and died. It had taken to being a little contrary, and my spark plug cleaning skills, which had seemed to do the trick at first, were not quite so fail-safe any longer. Anyway, we had arrived. Dismounting, we commenced a quiet assessment of the impressive white building in front of us.

"I wonder what he does all day," said Carol, irreverently.

Before we had time to hypothesise, an immaculately dressed servant came out to meet us and show us to the back of the house, where there was a huge terrace, overlooking a lovely garden. Peter Smart was casually dressed and eager to make us feel at home. He introduced us to his wife (whose name I forget) and we sat, while tea was served by a lovely young woman, again, beautifully turned out. (We were being effortlessly upstaged by the maids!)

After the niceties, we broached the reason for our visit and Mr. Smart listened sympathetically while Mrs. Smart looked concerned and ordered more tea. It was agreed that we had been misinformed. It had been an unfortunate and accidental deceit. Couldn't be helped. Of course our complaints were justified. No question. Only natural that we should be disappointed.

A week later, we collected a letter from Mrs. Smart, who apologised for her husband's absence and told us that she was perfectly capable of chatting to us in his stead, leading us out the terrace for more tea and polite conversation. After an appropriate period of mutual indulgence, we thanked her once more and left, happy to have the letter, sure that it would strengthen our case.

"Nice place," said Carol.

"Nice cakes," I added.

"What do we do with this?" she said, waving the envelope at me.

"Hand it to John and tell him to organise some flights."

"Still want to leave, then?"

Did I? "I think I do. How about you?"

"About time we did, I suppose."

The letter did the trick. It was settled, at last. We would receive vouchers for our flights and, to our delight, a rebate of most of the tax we had paid (thanks to the British system of taxation). The rebate would come to more than seven hundred pounds each – a small fortune in those days.

Our notice was finally, officially served, and we agreed to stay four more weeks in order to finish the last booklet. It was a victory, but it didn't feel like one. The mood I had was not of regret. Not quite. But of frustration. It would have taken so little to make us stay.

Fun and Farce at the French House

The French were off to Praslin, one of the larger of the secondary islands, for the weekend. This time we would accompany them.

It was time to make the most of our remaining weeks in the Seychelles. Marc arranged the flights and we met up at the airport to be shown to a small private plane with around twenty seats. If you've ever seen one, you'll know that the confidence they inspire is minimal, especially if you've grown up around planes, as I had.

There were eleven of us: Marc, Thierry, Emile, Marianne, Sven, Anka and Dragan (Lou had stayed home alone!), Rose and another Mauritian girl called Lena, Carol and I.

It wasn't the first time I'd been in a light aircraft, despite my father forbidding it, and I knew what to expect. That didn't mean that I would like it any better, though. Ah, the wholesome aroma of fuel! The gut-wrenching engine noise, with its layers of stutterings, to make you say your prayers and delve beneath your seat for a non-existent parachute. The experience was all too up-close and personal, making you more aware than you wanted to be that you were hundreds of metres above the Indian Ocean in a small metal tube with two cranking engines that had probably been kept in service with old bicycle parts.

The flight, however, would be mercifully short and, before I had time to think of more than a couple of hideous scenarios, we were descending for the landing.

"Look! There's Praslin," said Carol, wriggling in her seat.

"And La Digue," I added. It was much smaller and had no vehicles, only ox-carts for transportation.

"We can swim across," suggested Thierry, grinning.

It was common knowledge that the locals thought of the tourists who did such things as shark meat.

"What are they doing?" said Carol. "Look. On the airfield."

From our side of the aircraft we could see three dark figures pushing and dragging an enormous Aldabra turtle off the runway.

"Christ, wouldn't like to run over that one!"

"Wonder if they organise it for the tourists," I said. "Something to tell the folks back home." I used my American southern drawl. Carol gave me one of her looks.

The very smiley pilot touched down and we bounced along for a while before coming to a halt and breathing a communal sigh of relief.

It was another uncomfortably humid day and we commenced our walk to the French house. I can't remember which part of the island it was on, but it was isolated. The road was deserted, winding through the trees and then rising, without shade. We travelled light, with a rucksack between us. Rose had brought lemon tea. Up ahead, Sven walked with Lena, the very pretty

Mauritian girl, who had long shiny hair so black that it was almost blue, while a dejected but still overly optimistic Marianne kept us company, telling us about a film she had seen at the weekly showing laid on by the French Consul.

She was a pretty girl – I had noticed that the first time I'd seen her, with long, slender legs and a tiny waist. The problem was that she had no confidence. Carol called her 'Clingon' and I suppose that was an apt description in many ways. She was desperate to be liked and desperately dull to be with, as she spent most of her time moping.

"It was a brilliant film, you must see it!" said Marianne.

"How are you and Sven?" asked Carol, in self-defence, having endured yet another synopsis of a French film we'd never heard of. *Really? But it's international! You know it, I'm sure. It's about a...*

Even Rose was taken aback by the directness of the lovely Carol's assault.

"We're okay," Marianne replied, her rising intonation giving her away.

"You should ditch the bastard," continued my ever-loving bosom pal, Carol the truth-sayer.

Marianne had obviously been given similar advice by a number of other people.

"I know I should," she said, very quietly.

"Or play him at his own game."

"What do you mean?"

Rose and I pricked up our ears. This was more like it!

"Yeah. Marc hates Sven. Do a deal. Get your

-

188

-

own back!"

It was the hot topic for the rest of the walk. Childish? Yes. Predictable? Yes. Doomed to failure? Indubitably. But great fun. Marianne looked delighted, terrified and bewildered by turns. Carol took her arm and sorted her out.

The path continued to rise towards a bend on a summit, which hid what came next. There were giant boulders along the way and Marc took pictures. Sven kept ahead, never looking back, his intimacy with the new girl evident to all but Marianne.

Rose knew her well. "Lena is a piranha. If she wants something, she will chase it down and devour it. Even Sven doesn't know what she will do. The last boyfriend she had was married and now his wife has left him."

We contemplated this sober fact. And I pondered Rose's reference to Sven as 'it'.

"Maybe a bit of Lena damage will be good for the smarmy git," said Carol.

"You really don't like him, do you?" asked Marianne.

Her question would receive no reply.

"He is *nice*. He is *kind*. You only see the *bad* side," she insisted.

I could see that, if we weren't careful, Marianne would soon be wailing.

"Change the subject, for Christ's sake!" cried Carol. "I'm bored with hearing about the slimeball. Pull yourself together, can't you? Look! The house! Bugger me, it's a tin shack!"

Up another steep rise was a large structure,

with a sheltered terrace and a tin roof. There was a separate, smaller building, which apparently had a superior double bedroom. Sven and Marianne were supposed to be having that one.

Inside the main house, the heat was unbearable. We opened all the windows and I hung out our bedding, which was fungal-smelling and damp. The kitchen had been left with a sink full of washing up and there were cockroaches all over the place.

"Welcome to Paradise Hotel," said Marc, smirking and stooping to retrieve a large can of Doom.

Thierry did the rank washing up and Marc sprayed all the rooms. Emile unpacked the shopping the boys had lugged up the hill and then opened some beers, bringing them out to the terrace, where Marc had laid out some cushions. The place was not so bad in the end.

It was decided that we should have pasta – there was plenty in the storeroom. I was waiting for the boys to suggest that we prepare dinner, but I had misjudged them. Emile was a fantastic cook and the smells coming from inside soon drove us mad with appetite.

"I need onions!" He came out scowling. "No fucking onions!"

"Rose, Lena, make yourselves useful," said Marc, lying back in the shade.

"I don't mind going," said Lena.

"I'll come with you," said Sven.

Rose rolled her eyes and Marianne shrank to a slightly smaller version of herself.

There was a shop, of sorts, not far away and the three of them set off. Rose was trusted not to tell tales. How wrong they were!

It gave us time. Marc was delighted with our unsubtle plan and encouraged Marianne to go along with it. "You are a beautiful girl and you deserve a beautiful boyfriend."

"Watch yourself, Casanova!" said Carol.

"I am yours, my darling. You know this." He went down on one knee and Carol gave him the full dazzle of her ironic smile. She would not be taken in by such overt displays of gallantry.

"Get stuffed, you dodgy French philanderer!"

Rose came back without Lena or Sven.

"He told me to go," she said.

"Where are they?"

"I don't know."

Marianne let out a sob.

"Look, Marianne, if you don't make a stand, this bugger will ruin your life for a lot longer," said Carol.

We went over the plan again. He could not be allowed to triumph.

"Any onions?" asked Emile.

Rose handed him a bag.

The meal was delicious. Pasta with fish, onions, chilli and coconut. It was a new and brilliant experience. Emile had found a way to my heart, if only he could climb over my newly bloated stomach, that was. Just before we had finished, Lena and Sven sauntered back into the fold, electrifying the atmosphere and causing a number of sarcastic remarks, which they smilingly ignored. The supply of cold beer seemed endless, again, contractually supplied by the French government, no questions asked. So we drank and talked and played stupid party games, planning the activities for the next day, before we would have to fly back in the late afternoon.

At around two in the morning, Anka went to bed. Thierry disappeared at around the same time, and Dragan, looking very drunk, quite wrinkly and decidedly resigned to his wife's extra-marital athletics, went to sleep on the bench under the terrace shelter. Marianne was supposed to sneak out and go to Marc's room as soon as Sven had nodded off, after which we would wake him up and watch the drama unfold.

Of course, these things never work out.

It was Marianne who went to sleep, Sven and Lena disappeared, and Dragan woke us all up, screaming that he had been bitten on the head by a giant centipede. Anka emerged semi-clad, with one breast exposed and proceeded to calm her husband, waving us away.

"He's okay. Go back to bed. I'll get the poison out. Go! Shoo!"

Marc comforted a whimpering Marianne, and swore that when Sven came back he would kill him. Emile asked if I would like to go for a walk and, partly because I felt a tell-tale rumbling in my nether regions, partly because the whole thing was turning into some kind of restoration comedy piece, I declined.

"Fuck! Life is complicated when there aren't many people around," said Carol.

I knew what she meant – it was a claustrophobic environment, a microcosm of lust and frustration. Everyone knew everyone else, usually intimately. It was like shitting on your own doorstep, as Carol delicately declared, lying on the floor, under the table, as Marc stroked her belly with his foot.

At some point, we both managed to arrive once more in our allocated quarters. Carol went back to sleep, but I couldn't. The bed was still clammy, and once I started to listen to the sounds of the night, I could hear a thousand tiny scratches and wrigglings, imagining the life inside the walls, under the floor, inside the beams above our heads, in the wardrobes, in our bags, circumnavigating the gussets in our extra pants... Apart from that, I wondered what was going on in the other bedrooms and who was doing what with whom. I hovered between reality and delirium and passed out just as the sun rose, at around six.

Marc, Thierry and Emile were up early and off to the beach, where they had arranged to go snorkelling. They left a message to say they would be back for breakfast at 9.00. Needless to say, no one was awake when they returned. And nobody was about to volunteer to make breakfast.

The chirpy chappies made short work of setting out a spread that included pâté and proper French brie, with fresh bread bought at the shop. I was so impressed that I kissed Emile, whilst simultaneously sampling the *mousse de foie*. It was a bit messy, but he entered into the spirit of things.

We assembled, more or less hung over, and exquisitely grateful for our breakfast.

"Did you see anything?" I asked.

"A couple of sharks, some parrot fish, a ray," said Emile.

"Yeah, the ray was a bit friendly," laughed Thierry.

"I saw a stonefish and survived!" announced Marc. "Ugly bastard, hiding in the sand."

"Don't tell me," said Carol. "Let me guess. Did it look almost exactly like a stone?"

There were hoots of derision and Marc was forced to protest, much to the further amusement of the group.

They had brought back fish for our last meal – caught by Julian, the boy who had accompanied them with his boat. We would eat before we left. There was, however, not much time remaining to us.

"It's a holiday on Monday – we could stay another day and visit the Vallée de Mai," suggested Marc.

"Sounds good to me," I replied, looking around the table at all the nodding heads and relieved expressions. We had not done much. It would be good to make the most of the extra time, and so it was settled.

Coco de Mer and a Cautionary Tale

Anka and Dragan decided they would go back. They had seen the park on numerous occasions, and besides, Dragan would frighten away any wildlife we came across. His forehead was maroon and swollen into a tumour of a growth, which forced his left eye shut. Anka assured us that he would be fine. She had some pills at the house that would make him feel better. Dragan waved a hand in our general direction and acted as though it were nothing. I thought that, compared to the exploits of his adventurous wife, his injuries were probably of little concern to him.

It was strange to observe the way an older woman dealt with overt infidelity. Thierry had seemed edgy at the house, coming out for coffee and wandering around the garden, keeping his distance from Dragan. But it was as though nothing had changed between any of them, as far as Anka was concerned. Bizarre. Not that anyone was interested. We were all waiting for Sven to emerge from the bedroom, where Marianne had left him sleeping. Lena looked unbearably smug and stroked her perfect thighs under the table, making eyes at the other boys in turn as they provided her with coffee, fruit, cheese, anything she desired. Marianne sat with Carol – I think she felt protected by my formidable pal.

Eventually, Sven arrived with a face dying to be slapped. He was about to help himself to coffee when Marc stood up and took away the pot.

"You can get your own coffee," he said.

Sven shrugged his shoulders and went inside, coming back with a glass of milk and sitting next to Marianne, as though nothing in the world was wrong. Little more was said, although the atmosphere between Marc and Sven had never been so taut.

It was strange that none of the boys seemed to hold Lena responsible for what had happened. That was left to we girls.

After breakfast, Marc organised a lift with a local man and we sat in the back of his truck, bouncing along and feeling the worse for wear. Marianne and Sven were in the cab with the driver and it was clear that, yet again, she had forgiven her wayward boyfriend for his indiscretion. Lena acted as though nothing untoward had happened, and in the meantime, it was sickeningly pathetic to observe Thierry and Emile, fawning and flirting over her undeniable charms, announcing that she was the prettiest girl on the island, a catch for a lucky man, obviously hoping to cash in on their compliments.

"I think I'm going to puke up," Carol whispered to Rose and I.

Rose tittered and I said that I hoped it would be a well-aimed, projectile emission.

We were dropped off at the Vallée de Mai, which was one of the National Parks of the Seychelles and was home to the famous *coco de mer*. I was delighted when Carol, Marc and I found ourselves more or less on our own. It would be far less complicated and more relaxing, not to have to listen to the emotional wranglings of Moany Marianne and her faithless boyfriend's ill-advised romantic entanglements.

"You know that Emile is in love with you," Marc told me.

It wasn't something I had expected to hear.

"He thinks you don't like him."

I didn't know what to say. Did I like him?

"She'll come around," said Carol. "Either that, or she'll end up a prude and a spinster!"

"Well! Listen to Mata Hari… I haven't noticed you making much of a killing!" It was then that I noticed Marc's arm around my lovely friend's waist. "Oh!"

"You complete dunderhead!" said Carol, grinning.

"I can share my body, if you desire it," offered Marc.

Carol kicked him hard on the shin and we left him to hop along behind us, swearing in his mother tongue.

The place was like a giant botanical garden – the type that is found indoors at home. I have only ever visited such places on a much smaller scale. There is one in Cambridge, and when it was open, I used to go inside to warm up in winter, although the pungent smell of semi-rotting foliage was a bit off-putting. There was, however a real *coco de mer* tree there, so I already knew what to expect, although the ones above my head were three times taller, with voluminous fruit. In the Vallée de Mai, there were fantastical male and female 'genitalia' all around us. Everywhere we looked.

"Christ! It's like a pornographic set for a steamy triffid B movie. Fannies galore!"

"What about the phallus?" demanded Marc.

"Big and beautiful," said Carol.

"Thank you!" he foolishly replied.

It turned out that Marc could not hop quite so efficiently on his left leg.

The path through the park was narrow and we drank in the ever encroaching scenery: lush trees and plants which all but blocked out the sky and made a shady, dank bower which we inhabited half-tourist, half-adventurer. To enclose the jungle, to wrap it round with fences and lead paying guests through its tangled branches was at the same time, miraculous and absurd. We had been charged an entry fee and left to our own devices to wander around a patch of the island made separate for our benefit and the greater good of the Seychelles government coffers.

Marc took photos and told us more about Sven and Lena.

"She is a beautiful girl, but she has no morals."

It was instantly clear that Marc had been stung.

"She has been here for two years. The same time as me. She has a job at the French offices, due to her… influences."

"What do you mean?"

"She had an affair with one of the more prominent managers and, I think you heard, his wife found out and left him."

"How did she find out?" I asked, hoping for a juicy crime of passion scenario.

"It was Lena. She used to go to his apartment when his wife was away on business – a beautiful woman. She worked as a translator. Anyway, Lena was jealous and started to leave things in the apartment, or re-arrange things. Small at first. Eric didn't realise. But his wife became suspicious and looked out for things when she returned, hoarding the items she found, not mentioning anything to Eric. Lena must have known that Eric's wife suspected something, but she kept on. I don't know why."

"She sounds like a man-hater to me," chipped in Carol.

"You could be right. At least, she enjoyed it all, that much was clear."

"So, what happened?" We were sitting under one of the *coco de mer* trees, listening to the movement of the breeze in the fronds, the only people in the world. And Marc told us about the devastation of a marriage, a career and a future family, by the girl with the shiny blue-black hair and the long, long legs.

"I remember it. It was terrible. There was a party – Eric's birthday party. Lena was furious because she hadn't been invited. She screamed at him – some of us saw him in the car park after work. He tried to calm her, but she would not listen. Ella, his wife, was away. Not due back until the following afternoon, the day of the party. Lena had a key to the apartment and went over there, unbeknown to Eric. She hid her underwear

-
199
-

and some earrings under Ella's pillow."

"God! What a cow!"

"Yes. I think that Ella would have forgiven him until that point. But... after ... Well... She came home and told Eric that she was pregnant. He was so happy. They were both happy. And then she asked him whether he was seeing someone. And he made a big mistake. He told her that he had had an affair with a girl and that he was sorry; that it had ended, and that he loved Ella and wanted to spend his life with her. She was ready for his confession and, although she was deeply upset, I think she would have forgiven him."

"What a dick!"

"Yes. But I think you know what happened next?"

"No, tell us," I was hoping for a happy ending, even though I knew that they had broken up.

"It was during the party. Ella had gone to the bedroom to lie down for a while. She was tired from her journey, she said, and would be all right after a rest. Well, the next thing that happened was that she screamed. It was a terrible sound, rising above the music, so that people stopped, all of us, and looked at Eric. I think he knew. I could see it in his face. He went to her and there was a terrible row – I did not recognise their voices. Most of the guests left and I stayed behind with Eric's sister, who had come specially. Eric came out with his head in his hands. He kept saying, "It's over, it's over." And then moaning, "No!" He kept saying, "No!" His sister went in to

Ella. But it was no use. She would not stay. She left the next day. He followed her back to France, gave up his job. Last I heard, she was living with her mother, with the baby. Eric never contacted us. We don't even know where his is."

There was silence. It was a horrendous tale. We didn't know these people, but Marc did, and this fact made the whole thing far more poignant. As for Marc, he was exhausted, his head hanging down.

"Lena's a bitch of the first degree!" I said.

Carol shook her head for me to stop.

"It's easy to blame Lena," said Marc. "But the only person to blame was Eric. He was married and he was unfaithful. What is more, he lied to his wife. It was this she could not forgive."

"Does Sven know all this?" I asked.

"I don't think he knows the details. Why should he? Anyway, he has no love for Marianne. She is a fool. At least he does not hide the truth from her. She has herself to blame."

"You are very wise," said Carol. "For a stupid young Frenchman!"

This made Marc smile and soon we were marching along, asking what happened to Plastic Bertrand, who turned out not to be French at all, which was a bit like finding out that spaghetti bolognaise was not an Italian dish. We hurried, hoping that the van hadn't gone without us, and that the fish would soon be sizzling on the barbeque.

"Are you a womaniser?" I asked, cheerfully.

"I'm a nice guy!" said Marc. "Tell her, Carol!"

"Yeah. I've only ever known nice guys…" replied Carol.

I thought of Dave and I thought of Luc in France. It was true. They were both nice.

"About time we had some fun with some utter bastards, then!" I laughed.

Marc had his arm around Carol again and I wondered whether life would always be this complicated.

A Cultural Faux Pas

We got back home from Praslin the next day, glad to get away. It was time to do something simple, something that wouldn't have life-changing repercussions, so we cleaned the house. It was full of insects, as usual. When we had finished, we walked down the hill to our local shop and bought various things that all included an extra helping of weevil protein. Insect additives didn't bother us any longer; we had become used to such contaminations and thought nothing of finding creepy crawlies on our plates.

"I don't know why we don't just harvest our own fat free protein and be done with it," suggested Carol, but I could tell that her heart wasn't in it.

She said that she felt creative, and tried to make crispy cakes with melted chocolate, margarine and sugar, while I put a packet of *PolyBlonde* on my hair, the dye with the toxic fumes most likely to get you noticed. Neither of us had much success. The crispy cakes did not set, were not crispy and were unlike any cake known to man, my hair was partly blonde and partly orange-yellow-badger, as there had not been enough paste for full coverage. The same thing had happened to me in the past, the only difference being that I was near the chemists and could pop out for a top up.

"Do you want me to cut it?" asked Carol, licking her fingers.

"No thanks," I replied, knowing that anything Carol did to my hair would make it much, much worse. "I'll do it again when I get back to England.

"I've got a couple of boxes with me. You can have one if you like," she laughed.

What was left of the cake mixture was excellent for smearing on Carol's forehead and shoving up her nose, as it turned out.

The next day, we took the motorbike into Victoria and continued with our third and final booklet. At lunchtime, Millicent came to find us with a note requesting us to present ourselves in John's office at two o'clock.

"What's it about?" asked Carol.

"No say," replied Millicent, ambiguously, in Creole.

"Did you know your bum looks big in that dress?" said Carol.

This, she did not understand, although she knew full well that it was not intended as a compliment.

"*Vous beaucoup problem*," she laughed, sticking out her tongue and snorting her way out, for good measure. Carol was right, her bum looking quite enormous in her gathered floral skirt.

The unwelcome news that our infuriating co-worker had delivered made me remember what it had felt like years ago at school, when I had committed some minor breach of etiquette in junior school and had been sent to stand outside the headmistress's office. My pants had suddenly felt too big for me and threatened to fall down around my ankles. Now, my knees refused to hold still and I began to sweat.

Carol was unaffected, as she had more important things to do.

"Millicent's left her bag. Where's the sugar?"

John looked uncharacteristically serious when we arrived. Mr. Inconspicuous Observer was with him and I wondered whether our resignations were about to be turned down once and for all.

"Ah, ladies. Please come in," said Mr. IO, indicating two chairs and perching rather perkily on the corner of John's desk.

He was holding open a copy of our first booklet, which he turned around for us to see.

"Could you explain to me the meaning of this?"

I took the booklet and showed it to Carol, hoping for some insight into why he had asked us such a question.

"Oh," said Carol.

"What?" I said.

"Exactly," said Mr. Inconspicuous Observer, who had suddenly become more of a focal point than we wanted him to be.

Gradually, understanding dawned. In our enthusiasm to produce materials to interest our young students, we had forgotten that the Seychelles would not be the ideal place to present a lesson about the benefits of a drug with sedative qualities being administered to the people of a small island, where the government wished to assume absolute control over its people (at the time, the Seychelles was a one party republic). It was meant to be ironic, of course. The imbecilic expressions on the faces of the people and their list of frivolous pastimes, their moronic jobs, lack of motivation, and free education and health care – all this and more, was meant to inspire debate.

"It's not meant to be taken seriously," I said.

Mr. Inconspicuous Observer fixed me with a long-suffering smile. "Of course it isn't."

We heard a sharp squeak from Millicent's office. She had found her bag.

The booklets would have to be re-examined, censored and, if accepted, re-printed. We had messed up, John had not noticed, and so was deemed to have messed up too.

"Shitsticks," I said.

"Bollocky bollocks," replied Carol.

"Fuck a duck," murmured John.

It wasn't the end of the world, but it was a dodgy moment. We racked our brains and were pretty sure that there was no other controversial or overtly political material in the booklets. It was a week later before we found out that the revised version had passed their second reading and would be taken over to the island within the week. We were asked to accompany the delivery and make sure that the teachers knew what to do with them. It would be a challenge. I thought of the knitting circle, and of the silent disdain that would dampen any attempt at a lively presentation.

"They'll love them," said Carol. "They'll have to."

She had a point. It was a top-down system. You generally had to do as you were told. I would enjoy this far too much.

My presentation went without a hitch, amid lots of silent nodding and very little eye-contact. No objections were voiced in public, neither was there much enthusiasm. It was fair enough. After all, there had been no time for them to try out the materials in a classroom situation, no process of consultation or debate.

As yet, the materials would be optional. A supplement. Non-threatening. And the stuck up English teachers would soon be leaving. We would not be around for much longer and they knew it. I liked to think they would come around. That they would get some enjoyment and benefit from our efforts.

Apart from Rose and one of the French teachers, no one asked for my address or phone number.

A Deeply Embarrassing Blemish

In the meantime, I was getting more and more aware of an uncomfortable feeling when I sat down, especially on the bike. We'd be drumming along and suddenly, I'd cry out when we hit a bump.

"What's up?" Carol shouted.

"Nothing," I blared.

But, in the end, I could ignore it no longer and, with the help of a mirror, having politely refused the kind offer of help from my bosom buddy, I discovered a funny lump on my second most private part. After careful study, I was none the wiser. It was small and purple and hurt like hell.

"You've got piles!" announced Carol when we got back to the house.

"What are piles?" I asked, confused.

"Haemorrhoids."

"What?"

"Glow in the dark blisters that fall out of your bum when you strain too hard. Are you constipated?"

I was still contemplating the astounding accuracy of Carol's description of the foreign body I had discovered lodged in my nether regions. Was I constipated?

"A bit. But…"

"Probably the fact that we haven't eaten a proper vegetable since we arrived."

It was true that there was a paucity of leafy greens on the Seychelles, or carrots, or beans or…

"What can I do about it?"

"Well, in England, you could get some cream called 'Anusol'. I asked Dave to get me some once and he came back with 'Anbesol' which was a fat lot of good, as I wasn't teething at the time."

Staring had taken me over. What I needed was someone to tell me what to do. I didn't need to know what not to do. The lump on my bum had now assumed such massive importance that I could imagine floating away on it like Winnie the Pooh, attached to an enormous crimson balloon.

Carol noticed that I wasn't listening to her.

"Let's have a look," she said.

"Over my dead body!"

"I won't laugh."

"You will. And anyway, I'm not showing you."

"You'll have to show the doctor, then."

The unmitigated truth of this simple statement struck fear into my bottom. Where would I find one, and what would he or she be like? My doctor in England had been over sixty, infinitely patient and always ready with an optimistic prognosis. Never had I shown her my stinky bits. The thought of it clashed with her knee length tweed skirt and her careful perm, her support tights and her cashmere sweater. If I could not imagine baring all to Dr. Beresford, then how could I dare expose myself to a stranger in the middle of the Indian Ocean?

"Come on. No time like the present. Can you walk?" Carol held open the door. "More to the point, can you ride?" she said, dangling the keys.

"Ha, ha! Ouch!" Pain could be made so much worse by a combination of paranoia, terror and the cruel mockery of a friend.

We remembered that there was a Health Centre in Mont Flueri, which was not far. I clenched my buttocks together and gritted my teeth. Carol sang 'Sit Down Next to Me' all the way. It was very childish of her and I told her I was disappointed in her lack of imagination.

The Heath Centre turned out to be run by the Ministry of Health – would that be a good thing? It was a hospital, too. On the afternoon we arrived, there were around thirty mothers with their babies waiting on the steps. It didn't look as though we would be fitted in anytime soon.

Inside, there was a reception desk and the woman who was running it was surprised to see us. "Are you here for the immunisation programme?"

"No. Actually, I have a... I would like to see a doctor, please."

"Certainly. What is wrong with you, madam?"

Carol stepped forward.

"I have a problem with my bottom," I said quickly, whispering the last word.

"Ah! One moment, please." She picked up the telephone and a lady with short fair hair, a white coat and a stethoscope appeared almost immediately, equally as curious about the two westerners who had turned up on the wrong day, without a baby.

"Good afternoon," said the doctor.

"Hello. I'm terribly sorry, but we didn't know …"

"Would you like to come into the consultation room?"

I fled, leaving Carol in the waiting room, knowing that by the time I re-emerged, she would have made friends with everyone on the premises.

The doctor, who was Finnish, made short work of my unwanted bottom blemish. With the aid of a scalpel and a few kind words of encouragement, she sliced it off and said that I should wear a sanitary towel for a few days.

"No white trousers."

It was hard to know whether she was trying to be funny.

"Thank you," I said, hardly believing that it had all been so simple. "Do I pay you?"

"No. All is free. Seychelles health service is paid by the government." The doctor held out her hand, and I shook it.

"Do you want to see your haemorrhoid?"

I told her she could keep it, if she liked, which made her laugh, a bit.

It was impressive that such a small nation should aspire to a level of health care that aimed to provide free and expert attention at the drop of a hat. It was not the only time I would use the health centre, and I was extremely grateful for it.

We rode back gingerly. Carol decided to treat me to a heartfelt rendition of 'The First Cut is the Deepest' and I must admit that she did it in a way I had never heard before.

The next day, I felt much better.

"Poor little haemorrhoid! Sliced off and flushed away."

"I hope it comes back and attaches itself to your nose!"

"I wonder if his little friends are missing him..."

I should have known better than to listen.

Uninvited Guests

We decided to go out to a restaurant. We hadn't done so until then, mostly because there were hardly any places to go, apart from hotels. We had eaten at the Pirate's Arms a few times, but it was time to be more adventurous. Something more authentic was what we craved, so we asked around and were told about the *Marie Antoinette*, just outside Victoria.

"You go first," I begged Carol, standing behind her in the darkness at the top of the path down to the road.

"Christ on a bike! Give me the bloody broom."

She walked ahead as I prepared myself to run the gauntlet, wheeling the bike down the path between two ever-expanding bushes. The spiders spun their webs after dark, thick enough to twang. In the morning, it was just light enough to see, as we went down to catch the bus for work, but in the darkness… well, the thought of it made me feel sick with worry.

"All clear, my lovely tart-face," called Carol.

I put on the bike's headlights in case she had missed one and edged my way down to join her.

"Thanks."

"That's all right, me duck."

This was what the ladies at the cafeteria had always said when we were at Keele university. It made me smile to remember.

We tootled along the coastal road, were

attacked by dogs twice, and nearly ran over a group of children in the middle of the road – just a normal trip. The restaurant was easy to find and looked very busy indeed.

We parked and went inside, where we were shown to a table by a young, smiling waitress. In a much larger adjoining room, it looked as though there were a wedding reception going on.

"Wow! Look at all that food!"

All along one side of the room was an enormous buffet. The waitress handed us a menu.

"Where's the toilet?" Carol asked.

"I will accompany you, madam," replied the waitress.

"I'll come too!"

She looked just a little suspicious, but led us into the reception room, keeping to the side and indicating the door we were after.

The bride was dressed exactly as a traditional British bride would be. She wore a dress with a tight, scrolled bodice with a many-layered skirt, flaring from the waist, and had a tiara with a veil thrown back over her tight bun. She was young, very dark-skinned, and utterly beautiful. Next to her, sat her husband, young too, and wearing a dark, slightly over-generous suit with a flamboyant waistcoat and a deep red rose for a buttonhole. He exuded confidence and pride.

I came out of the toilet to find that Carol was talking to what might have been the mother of the bride, as she was an enormous African woman with a proprietary air, who bore no resemblance to the delicately featured Asian groom. I watched for a moment or two, wondering what on earth they could be talking about, but forgetting that Carol was a master at striking up a conversation with anyone in the world, in any situation. Soon, she was undergoing a tip-toeing initiation in one of the local dances, attempting to catch the rhythm of the music whilst moving feet and hips in a circular gyration. I got the camera from Carol's jacket and snapped away. By this time, the groom had noticed the foreign bodies on the dance floor and I saw him turn to his bride, who nodded, grinning with all the joy of a delighted newly wed. *Get them out of here! Do something! Gut the gatecrashers!* As he approached, I wanted to run. There could be no positive outcome. We would be evicted, slung out, humiliated and not be able to order our meal. My stomach growled and I rose up to my full height.

"Good evening, Miss," said the groom, bowing slightly. "May I?"

May you what? And before I could think of an answer, he led me onto the dance floor amid a round of applause from the guests, who must have been highly amused by my attempts at a Seychellois boogie. It didn't seem to matter that we were strangers from a far off land, where mottled skin and two-tone hair were in fashion; we were welcomed and made to feel a part of the celebrations, as if it were the most natural thing in the world.

The complex beat, irregular and hypnotic, soon took me over and I believed that I was moving brilliantly, carried away by my obvious talent for dance. It wasn't long before other guests joined us, nodding and smiling, urging me on. I was a dancing queen, young and sweet, only thirty-ee! Carol was now shimmying up and down the mother of the bride in a more or less obscene show of dance floor competitiveness, and my partner had taken my hand to lead me in the most unusual rock and roll I'd come across. It was a hoot. I was hooked. I was off-balance. I was down. I was up again!

"Isn't it brilliant!" I said, as I swung past Carol.

"It's the dog's bollocks!" she shouted.

"What is 'dog's bollocks'?" asked my partner, moments later, when the music had finished.

"It means 'excellent'," I told him, "'top-notch'!" I congratulated myself on my super-slick avoidance of a direct translation of such an explicit idiom.

"Ah!" His eyes widened in approval, as he reached down and clutched his testicles, before extending his other hand to introduce himself. "My name is Sidney and my wife, Marie and I, would like to invite you to join us."

We found that there was no way of declining, not that we had any intentions of seriously trying, so we joined the party at the head table and were served a sumptuous feast of food so colourful and fragrant that it brought tears to my eyes. What had we been missing!

Marie didn't say much, but she oozed goodwill, always guiding the best dishes towards us, watching good-naturedly as we tried not to commit a *faux pas*.

"Do you think the food is spiked?" I whispered to Carol.

"Pass the fritters," she replied.

"What are you drinking?"

"Tastes like Piña Colada. Got it from the bar. It's free. Want one?"

Before I could stop her, she had called over a waiter and ordered one for me. The music continued, at intervals. We ate, drank and danced in steady rotation, until late into the night. I conversed freely in English, Creole and everything in between. It had been an evening to remember. Unexpected fun - the best kind.

Our hosts ordered a taxi to take us home, asking for our address and saying that someone would drop off our motorbike the next day. The bride and groom thanked us for our company. The mother in law hugged Carol and pinched her cheeks, saying she was welcome at her home anytime, handing over her son's business card and saying she should call whenever she needed anything.

The taxi driver helped us to our door and we gave him the rest of the money in our purse, whispering loudly and shushing each other, hilariously.

I woke up in Carol's bed, with the sun burning my cheek, to hear her at the door, speaking to a man who was unloading our bike from his truck. I had no headache. Only memories of fun and laughter. It was miraculous.

"Coffee?"

"Coming!"

"What a great night!" I burst into song, and Carol told me that she would kill me if I didn't shut up.

"Where did you sleep, you gorgeous tart?" I asked, still buoyant.

"In the bathroom."

"Why?"

"No idea. But it wasn't very nice."

We went back to the *Marie Antoinette* once more before we left Seychelles, but it was not the same. In the darkness of the candle-lit restaurant, unable to identify the extent of the weevil component amongst the rice, all I could think about was the gaiety of the wedding party, the shining eyes of the guests and the complicated rhythm of the music.

"More curry?" asked Carol.

"What is it?"

"No idea."

"No thanks."

"Are you thinking about the party?" she asked. I saw that she was, too. "Think I'll say yes when I get back," she added, almost casually.

She meant to Dave. It had been inevitable. It was the right thing, probably. But it still made my heart stop just for an instant, as I looked into her eyes and knew that this adventure might very well be the last we would experience together.

Goodbye Seychelles

There would be a film showing at the British Consul building in Victoria in the middle of the week. We would be leaving soon and so we decided to do whatever presented itself to us, in the meantime.

Carol read from a programme: "Eight o'clock, *One Flew over the Cuckoo's Nest*, drinks to start, drinks to finish."

"Might as well go. It's free."

Penny and Dick would be there. They went regularly, and I imagined having to listen to the endless anecdotes about Dick and his misadventures whilst trying not to wring Penny's neck for letting the whole of womankind down. It would be difficult, but for a good film, it would be worth it. We'd both seen it before. I was looking forward to Jack Nicholson's award-winning performance, but most of all, I wanted to see nurse Ratched again.

The bike eventually fired up and we arrived a little late. There was just time to say hello to our friends, pour ourselves a glass of wine and grab a few nibbles, before the lights went down and the opening credits rolled. I glanced sideways at Carol and was glad we'd come.

I'd always been able to jump into a film and tonight was no exception. When nurse Ratched first appeared on the screen, I was there with the inmates, the hairs on the back of my neck standing up, willing Randle McMurphy to be wary, to realise the extent of her cunning. Of course, the irony of knowing what was going to happen worked me into a frenzy and by the time the hero had tried to strangle the vile, yet hugely provocative dictator, paying for his courage with his sanity, I watched the Chief stride away with tears in my eyes.

The lights went up and I looked at Carol.

"She's so like you!" she said.

"Who?"

"Nurse Ratched."

This assessment of my character wrong-footed me, and I had no witty retort to hand. It was one of those moments when you almost feel that a comment has some truth to it, the realisation of which disturbs you to the core with its unsavoury implications.

"Only joking, you dunderhead!"

I relaxed, relief washing over me.

"Not!"

Violence would have been inevitable, had I not been interrupted.

"Did you read the book?" It was Penny. She was wearing an orange jacket of exquisite bad taste.

I hadn't read the book. Penny had. "He rips her clothes off in the book," she told me, grinning, winking at Dick.

I wished she hadn't said it. I felt the integrity of the film disintegrate. I wished...

"Come and have a fishpaste sandwich," said Carol.

"Are you all right?" asked Dick.

"She's fine," replied my bosom buddy, "just a bit of morning sickness."

We didn't stay long. Outside in the cooler night air, I recovered my composure, wondering how I had been affected so deeply by a night out at the cinema.

"We can book our flights tomorrow, if you like," said Carol.

"Yes. I'd like to," I replied.

"Right. But, just stay over there for now, okay?"

"Why?"

"You don't want to see this."

"What?"

"Trust me."

I tried, but failed. On the right wing mirror of the bike there was an enormous spider, its legs splayed out in a perfect circle of horror, its body pulsing up and down.

"Don't kill it!" I said.

Carol looked at me. "I won't," she replied. She covered it with her scarf and shook it out into the bushes. "Let's go, gorgeous!"

I drove back, aware of Carol sitting behind me and hoping that nothing else was hitching a ride. I was ready to leave the Seychelles.

The following day, we picked up the vouchers John had reserved for us and found that we were able to exchange our flights with British Airways for half-way-round-the-world tickets, with stopovers at Bangkok, Singapore and Hong Kong.

Our work in the Seychelles was finished and we wanted to say our goodbyes. We met up in The Pirate's Arms on the morning of our departure. Rose clasped me to her and, with tears in her eyes, said she would miss me, handing over a large parcel containing tinned cheese, homemade cakes and winter socks, bearing the Manchester address of her brother. The French contingent waved us off, settling in for the day, loud and jovial. Only Marc seemed to really care that we were leaving. Anka sent her love, unable to come in person. Sven and Marianne were not there. John arrived to take us to the airport, mild-mannered and pragmatic, as ever. We asked him to stop off at the post office, where we paid a small fortune for Rose's weighty parcel to be sent.

"That's very kind of you," said John, smiling.

He helped us with our luggage and took his leave, thanking us for our hard work and wishing us happiness in our future lives.

"Bangkok here we come!" cried Carol.

We had our freedom back and would see some more of the world, after all!

The End

Author's note: I hope you enjoyed 'Stranded in the Seychelles'. If you would like to leave a review on Amazon, please do. I always appreciate it.

There are two other books in the Bev and Carol series, each of them stand-alone adventures: 'One Summer in France' and 'Bunny on a Bike'. Here is the first chapter of 'One Summer in France', when Bev and Carol are younger, midway through their university degree courses and ready for the trip of a lifetime:

Chapter One

Stolen Milk and Toenail Clippings

It was unbelievable, but apparently true. The university would contribute towards an obligatory three-month stay in France during the summer break for those students taking French as part of their degree course. Hard cash was on offer for a holiday adventure.

'Hang on a minute. Who exactly told you about this?' I asked Carol.

'Andy did,' she replied, looking up from her nail clipping.

'Andy?' (I had never seen such long toenails).

'Yeah, Andy. James' best mate. You know, the posh one with greasy hair and an annoying laugh.'

'Oh, that Andy!' I didn't really have any idea whether something that Andy said might be true. I didn't know him that well.

I became aware that Carol was cutting her nails on the baking tray that I had used to make shortbread only the day before.

'What did you do with the biscuits I made?' I asked, already knowing the answer would not please me.

'I ate the last few. Needed the tray.'

'Did you save me one?'

'Sorry, no. They weren't very nice, anyway.'

Carol filled the kettle and wandered, barefoot and newly clipped, out of the kitchen and back to her room to find tea bags. Anything you wanted to hold on to had to be kept well away from the communal kitchen.

I picked up the tray, emptied the gruesome contents into the bin and inserted it into the stack of washing up.

Looking out over the trees and fields on the edge of the campus, which seemed to be bathed in the luminous glow of new optimism, I thought of Dylan Thomas and his early poetry, when he was 'green and golden' and before he started 'raging against the night', and then I thought of not having to spend the summer on top of the Long Mynd surrounded by boring glider pilots, or in my father's ridiculous house in Milton Keynes, miles from my home town of Bridgnorth, where my friends would be having a great time without me. France spread itself out before me like a wanton hussy, luring me away from dutiful daughterly obligations and unpaid summer chores.

I had a moment of guilt. A second's hesitation. But, hey! Life was for living! Here I was, my latest assignment practically written, although not actually set out on paper, my second year coming to an end, my roots newly bleached and my legs devoid of bristles, thinking about the prospect of bombing off to France with my best pal on an all-expenses-paid holiday which would count as part of my studies.

'Yes!' I said. 'Yes, yes, yes!'

'Quick. Get some milk, can you?' said Carol, coming back more speedily than she had left.

'Which one is yours?' I asked, springing into action, bending down to look in the fridge and trying not to breathe.

Carol gave me a sub-zero glare, which meant that I was being a birdbrain, again. (We rarely bought milk.)

'How about this one?' I suggested.

'Give it a sniff first,' she advised, dunking the teabags and squeezing them between two forks, 'but for God's sake hurry up!'

'Yuk!' I felt the skin inside my nostrils shrivel.

'Must be Mike's,' Carol said, reasonably.

'This one smells fine – here!' I went to the door and looked up and down the corridor, trying not to look at the red floral carpets.

Carol sloshed milk into the mugs and handed it back to me.

'I'll get a bottle later,' I mumbled, putting it back in the fridge and noticing the sticker on the side, which read: 'Buy your own bloody milk!'

'My place or yours?' asked Carol, disregarding my empty promise.

'I've got rice pudding. Have you got jam?' I asked, helping myself to two spoons and the last couple of clean bowls.

Our rooms were large, with wide windows that looked out over the campus. I had queued for hours at the beginning of term to get into Horwood Hall, which was by far the best hall of residence on campus, and had managed to secure two of the best ones for Carol and myself. The lady at the Accommodation Office had been very kind, understanding that Carol was, to all intents and purposes, stuck on the motorway and unable to be there in person. She handed me two sets of keys and said that Carol should come and sign in when she arrived. Sorted!

We sat on my bed and listened to the argument that had started up in the kitchen. Carol grinned and I bit my lip, waiting for a knock at the door.

'Hide the mugs!' I hissed, but Carol did not oblige. She wanted trouble, I could tell.

Alison banged several times on the door and shouted, 'You selfish cows! Do you think I don't know it was you!'

We looked innocently at each other and Carol went to the door.

'Hello, Alison. Is there something wrong? Has somebody died?' She looked past her uninvited guest.

'You took my milk, again!'

'It's a communal fridge, for goodness sake,' said Carol, sipping her tea and, by definition, Alison's milk. 'You can borrow ours when you run out. Give and take, Alison. Give and take.'

Alison adjusted her glasses and folded her arms. She was smiling, but it was not in a friendly way. 'Agreed. If you ever bought any milk, that is! Until you do, it's my bloody milk! The milk belongs to me. It is not, as you point out, *communal*. Get it!'

I thought that I would mitigate the situation. 'I'll get a bottle later, if you like?' I offered, feeling the weight of our crime and a certain amount of regret.

Alison would not listen. She puffed and fumed and stormed off, muttering something about not being able to talk to people like us.

'Right!' said Carol, who could instantly put aside anything that did not interest her. 'Let's get down to the Finance Office and grab ourselves some of this lovely holiday lolly before it all disappears.

****

There are direct links to all my books on Amazon,
via my blog: baspicer.blogspot.fr

Made in the USA
Coppell, TX
14 November 2021